SECOND EDITION

Windows 8.1: Out of the Box

Mike Halsey

Beijing · Cambridge · Farnham · Köln · Sebastopol · Tokyo

Windows 8.1: Out of the Box, Second Edition

by Mike Halsey

Printed in the United States of America.

Published by O'Reilly Media, Inc., 1005 Gravenstein Highway North, Sebastopol, CA 95472.

O'Reilly books may be purchased for educational, business, or sales promotional use. Online editions are also available for most titles (*http://my.safaribooksonline.com*). For more information, contact our corporate/institutional sales department: 800-998-9938 or *corporate@oreilly.com*.

Editor: Rachel Roumeliotis
Production Editor: Dan Fauxsmith
Proofreader: O'Reilly Publishing Services

Cover Designer: Karen Montgomery
Interior Designer: David Futato
Illustrator: Robert Romano

October 2013:   Second Edition

Revision History for the Second Edition:

2013-10-18:   First release

See *http://oreilly.com/catalog/errata.csp?isbn=9781491946107* for release details.

ISBN: 978-1-491-94610-7

[LSI]

With thanks to Richard Gilbane, ever loyal and supportive.

Table of Contents

Preface

Audience

This book is for anybody who is coming to use Windows 8.1 for the first time, perhaps through purchasing a new computer or a first tablet, and who wants to know how to get the very best user experience from this new version of Windows.

Assumptions This Book Makes

This book assumes that you have a little prior computing experience and that you understand the basics, such as how to use a mouse and keyboard. You should not need any more experience than this. It is probable that in the past, you have used a computer only for light tasks such as email and surfing the web.

Contents of This Book

This book will guide you through using Windows 8.1 by focusing on the things you will most likely want to do with your Windows 8.1 computer. These include getting on the Internet, using email and web pages safety, importing and editing digital photographs from your camera, and making sure your children are protected when they're online.

Conventions Used in This Book

The following typographical conventions are used in this book:

Italic
> Indicates new terms, URLs, email addresses, filenames, and file extensions.

This icon signifies a tip, suggestion, or general note.

This icon indicates a warning or caution.

Safari® Books Online

 Safari Books Online is an on-demand digital library that delivers expert content in both book and video form from the world's leading authors in technology and business.

Technology professionals, software developers, web designers, and business and creative professionals use Safari Books Online as their primary resource for research, problem solving, learning, and certification training.

Safari Books Online offers a range of product mixes and pricing programs for organizations, government agencies, and individuals. Subscribers have access to thousands of books, training videos, and prepublication manuscripts in one fully searchable database from publishers like O'Reilly Media, Prentice Hall Professional, Addison-Wesley Professional, Microsoft Press, Sams, Que, Peachpit Press, Focal Press, Cisco Press, John Wiley & Sons, Syngress, Morgan Kaufmann, IBM Redbooks, Packt, Adobe Press, FT Press, Apress, Manning, New Riders, McGraw-Hill, Jones & Bartlett, Course Technology, and dozens more. For more information about Safari Books Online, please visit us online.

How to Contact Us

Please address comments and questions concerning this book to the publisher:

O'Reilly Media, Inc.
1005 Gravenstein Highway North
Sebastopol, CA 95472
800-998-9938 (in the United States or Canada)
707-829-0515 (international or local)
707-829-0104 (fax)

We have a web page for this book, where we list errata, examples, and any additional information. You can access this page at *http://bit.ly/ windows_8dot1*.

To comment or ask technical questions about this book, send email to *bookquestions@oreilly.com*.

For more information about our books, courses, conferences, and news, see our website at *http://www.oreilly.com*.

Find us on Facebook: *http://facebook.com/oreilly*

Follow us on Twitter: *http://twitter.com/oreillymedia*

Watch us on YouTube: *http://www.youtube.com/oreillymedia*

How to Contact the Author

Mike has an open mailbag and always welcomes questions and comments from readers. He sincerely hopes you have enjoyed this book and that you will consider reviewing it online.

Please visit Mike's website at: *http://www.thelongclimb.com*.

Find Mike on Facebook: *http://www.facebook.com/HalseyMike*

Follow Mike on Twitter: *http://www.twitter.com/HalseyMike*

Watch Mike's help and how-to videos: *http://www.youtube.com/ HalseyMike*

Acknowledgments

With thanks to Sander Berkouwer for your valuable contribution.

Using Windows 8.1

Windows 8.1 is very different from previous versions of Windows from Microsoft, primarily in that it has a new look that's been redesigned to be easy to use with touch as well as with a mouse and keyboard. It's been greatly simplified too, so for the first time it's no longer necessary to understand how small and fiddly drop-down menus work, or to understand how to control programs using complicated desktop menus where you have to manage and juggle multiple programs on your screen at one time.

Now we have an update to Windows 8 in the form of Windows 8.1. It's free, downloadable from the Windows Store, and contains many features and improvements.

Windows 8.1 can be operated by a keyboard and mouse without problems, though with a touchscreen computer or tablet you will benefit from the richest experience.

Everything has changed to make it not just easier to find and control documents, apps, and programs, but to make overall control of Windows and your settings simpler. At last, you don't need to be a technical user to get the best out of using Windows.

When you use Windows 8.1 on your computer, laptop, or tablet for the first time, you'll notice how different it looks and works. This new look makes it easier for you to see what's going on in your online life at a glance: Live Tiles can show you information about your email, calendar, instant messaging, social networking, sports, news, and much more, all without ever leaving the new Start screen.

In this chapter, I'll demonstrate what these new interface elements are and how to use them.

Top Tips from This Chapter

1. You can open menus and options on the Start screen by swiping with your finger from any edge of the screen.

2. Move your mouse to the corners of the screen to display options and menus.

3. On your keyboard, you can hold down the *Windows Key* in the bottom left of the keyboard and press *Z* or *C* to open menus and options.

The Start Screen Versus the Desktop: What You Need to Know

I've already mentioned the new interface in Windows 8.1, the Start screen. The *traditional* Windows desktop still exists though, so you can still use software you're used to in Windows 7.

 Windows RT is slightly different from Windows 8.1 in that you cannot install Desktop programs. RT still comes with a desktop and pre-installed copies of Microsoft's Office programs Word, Excel, Power-Point, OneNote, and Outlook. Also, the desktop utilities like Paint, Notepad, and the Calculator still exist there. You cannot install more desktop software on a Windows RT computer though.

There is a new style of program in Windows 8.1, however, called an App. These apps (or applications) run full screen and are easier and friendlier to use than desktop programs. Windows 8.1 comes preinstalled with many apps for email, calendar, news, and so on, and you can download many more from the new Windows Store. You will see the *Store* tile on the Start screen.

Windows 8.1 apps come from the new Windows Store. This is an easy to find and easy to use way of getting the apps you want, a task that has been difficult in the past with desktop software that was scattered across hundreds of individual websites. I will show you how to use the Windows Store and install apps and programs in Chapter 4.

Starting Windows 8.1

When Windows 8.1 starts, you will see the lock screen (Figure 1-1). This displays the time and date and can also show extra information, including how many emails you have and what your next calendar appointment is. You can also use this lock screen as a digital photo frame, and I'll show you how to set this up in Chapter 3.

 You open the lock screen by swiping upward on the screen with your finger if you have a touch display, or by pressing any key on the computer's keyboard.

Figure 1-1. The Windows 8.1 lock screen

When you first started using your computer, you may have set a password for your user account. If you did, you will be asked for this before you can unlock the computer. You can also create a numerical (PIN) password for Windows 8.1 or use a picture password. I will show you how to do this in Chapter 13.

To switch between using a standard password, PIN, or picture if you have one set, click/touch *sign-in-options* at the sign-in screen when asked for your password.

Finding Your Way Around the Start Screen

The Start screen (Figure 1-2) in Windows 8.1 is based around square and rectangular colored blocks called Tiles. When clicked or tapped, each one starts an app. The app will then perform a specific task, such as sending and receiving email, viewing web pages, editing photographs, or playing a game. The Start screen pans left to right across your screen.

 Swipe left and right with your finger to pan across the Start screen. If you are using a mouse, you will see a scroll bar at the bottom of the screen when you move the mouse. Click/Touch and drag this left and right to look around the Start screen. You can also use the scroll wheel (up and down) on your mouse to move left and right on the Start screen.

Figure 1-2. The Windows 8.1 Start screen

As you look around the Start screen, you will see that some Tiles change occasionally to display text or images. These are Live Tiles, which give you information from inside the app or show you what is new or changed, such as giving you a message.

These messages can include details of new emails or social network messages, informing you of the number of updates that are available for your apps in the Windows Store or giving you news headlines.

You can rearrange Tiles on the Start screen by right-clicking or touching and holding one of them. This puts you into customization mode, where you can drag tiles around and drop them into new locations, which can help you organize them to best suit you. I will show you how to organize the Start screen in Chapter 4.

 When you drag a Tile between groups, you will see a colored vertical bar appear. If you drop the Tile onto this bar, you can create a new group. This can be useful to separate apps. For example, you can separate games, websites, and so on.

Using the Charms

The Start Button from previous versions of Windows (sometimes known as the Windows Orb) had the function of helping you find and run programs. In Windows 8.1, you can find the Start button in the new Charms menu (Figure 1-3). This pops out from the right side of the screen and contains icons for useful tasks in Windows 8.1.

You can open the Charms Menu by swiping in from the right of the screen with your finger or pressing *WindowsKey+C* on your keyboard (the WindowsKey is the key at the bottom left of your keyboard with the Windows logo on it). To open the Charms Menu with a mouse, move your mouse to the bottom right or the top right corner of the screen.

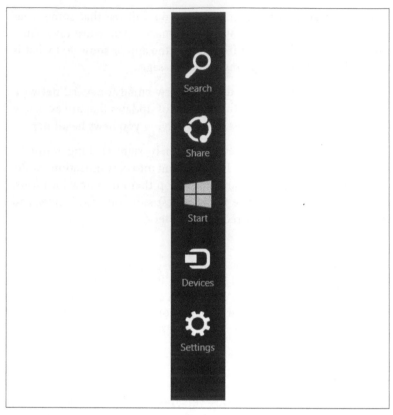

Figure 1-3. The Charms menu

On the Charms Menu, you will find the following options:

- *Search* opens the search panel so you can find apps, documents, and Windows 8.1 Settings.

- *Share* allows you to share text, pictures, and more between Windows 8.1 apps and also save pages from apps and the Internet to read later.

- *Start* returns you to the Start screen; this is also available by pressing the Windows Key on your keyboard or the Windows button on your tablet computer.

- *Devices* allows you to print documents, web pages, and information from apps, use external display projectors, and other hardware devices.

- *Settings* displays the Windows Settings and controls as well as displaying controls for the currently running app.

 You can also search for apps, settings, and files and even Internet content by typing directly at the Start screen. You do not need to open the Search panel.

Using the App Bar

If you have used an earlier version of Windows, you might know that pressing the *right* mouse button can bring up a menu of options associated with an icon or program. In Windows 8.1 apps and on the Start screen, this *right-click* now displays the App Bar.

The App Bar (Figure 1-4), which is also available by swiping up from the bottom of your screen with your finger or swiping down from the top, contains menu options that are available for that app.

To open the App Bar with your mouse, right-click in an app or on the Start screen. To open the App Bar from your keyboard, press *WindowsKey+Z*.

These options are equivalent to drop-down menus in Windows desktop programs and can perform many functions, each of which depends on the context of where you are and what you are doing.

Figure 1-4. The App Bar in Windows 8.1

 To perform an action on a Tile on the Start screen, such as hiding it from the Start screen completely (I will show you how to organize apps and tiles on the Start screen in Chapter 4), you can right-click/touch on the Tile with your mouse, or touch and hold it with your finger, and the App Bar will appear with options for actions you can perform on that Tile. You can open the App Bar from your keyboard by pressing *WindowsKey+Z* in any app or from the Start screen.

If you want to open a menu in an app or on the Start screen, you will do this from the App Bar. This is where all the controls for apps can be found.

Finding All the Apps in Windows 8.1

Not all of the apps and software in Windows 8.1 will appear on the Start screen. For example, you may have chosen to hide a Tile to keep your Start screen tidy, or perhaps you don't use it regularly. Also, newly installed apps and programs won't appear on the Start screen, so if you want to pin them there you will need to do so from within the All Apps view.

You can see all of the apps that are installed in Windows 8.1, including Windows desktop programs. When you move your mouse around your screen, a small down arrow will appear near the bottom left corner. You can click this to open the All Apps view. If you are using touch, swipe upward on the Start screen to open the All Apps view.

You can return to the Start screen by swiping downward in the All Apps view with your finger, clicking the small up arrow near the bottom left of your screen, or pressing the Windows key.

In the All Apps view (Figure 1-5), you will see every app and all of the desktop software that is installed on the computer. The apps that appear on the left of the screen, and the desktop software on the right, are organized into clearly labelled categories to make things easy to find. You can move left and right in the All Apps view as you would on the Start screen. You can change how your apps and programs are arranged in the All Apps view by clicking the *by Name* link in the top left of the screen.

Figure 1-5. Finding all apps in Windows 8.1

If you want to pin an app or program back on the Start screen, *right-click* (touch and hold) it and select *Pin to Start* from the App Bar.

Switching Between Running Apps in Windows 8.1

You can press the Windows Key on your keyboard or the Start Charm at any time to return to the Start screen, but you can also switch between apps by dragging the previous app from the left of the screen with your finger. With a keyboard, you can use the *WindowsKey +Tab* keys to switch between running apps.

Docking Apps to the Left or Right of the Screen

When you drag an app in from the left of the screen with your finger, you will see a vertical bar appear in the left quarter or right quarter of the screen, depending on where you are dragging it at that point. Dropping an app when you see this bar will *dock* it to the far left or the far right of the screen (Figure 1-6). You can also drag the currently displayed app downward from the top center of the screen to dock it to the left or right of the screen.

Figure 1-6. Arranging apps on screen in Windows 8

To close the currently running app, drag it downward from the top center of the screen with your mouse or finger, and throw it off the bottom of the screen.

If you then return to the Start screen by pressing the Windows Key, the next app you run will fill the remaining space, so you have two apps side by side. You can drag the vertical bar separating them left and right to switch the focus from one app to the other, or to move one app off the screen completely.

To dock apps side by side using a mouse (this also works with touch), drag the app from the top center of the screen toward the center of the screen. You will see the app change to a thumbnail image. You can now drag this thumbnail to the left or right of the screen and drop it when you see the vertical *dock* bar appear.

If you have a large enough screen (this just won't work if you don't), you can arrange up to four apps on screen. When you are running two apps side by side, if you launch a third app it will appear as a thumbnail between them (Figure 1-7). You can drag it left or right to replace the running app there or, if you hover between the running apps you will see a space open into which you can drop it.

Figure 1-7. You can have up to four apps on screen at any time

Logging Out Of and Locking Windows 8.1

If several people use Windows 8.1 on your computer and you want to switch to a different user, you can do this by clicking or touching your user icon and name in the top right of the Start screen. This will bring up a menu with three options (Figure 1-8).

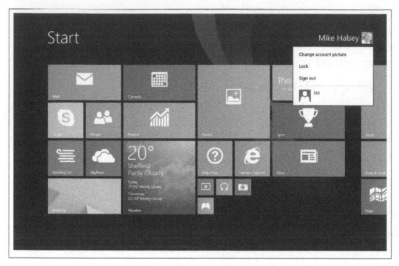

Figure 1-8. The User Menu in Windows 8.1

 If you want to change your password, you can do this from the *Accounts* page in *PC Settings*. Click/Touch the *Settings* Charm and then click *Change PC Settings* to access the options.

- *Change Account Picture* will allow you to choose a new picture for your account from images that you have on your computer.

- *Lock* will lock the computer so that a password, PIN, or picture password is needed to sign in again. This is useful if you are leaving your computer unattended for a while.

- *Sign-Out* will sign out of your account so that others can use the computer.

If you have multiple user accounts set up in Windows, perhaps for different members of your family (I will show you how to set these up in Chapter 11), these people will also appear in the user list when you click/touch your name in the top right of the Start screen. You can switch directly to another user by clicking their icon (you will *not* be logged out). This means that if you have any files or documents open that you have not saved, they might be lost if another user then shuts the computer down. They will be warned, however, by Windows 8.1 if another user is still logged in when they turn the computer off.

Using Touch Gestures in Windows 8.1

I have already shown you some of the touch gestures you can use in Windows 8.1, including touching a Tile to open it and touching and holding for a second to select it.

There are other gestures you can use, including two-finger pinch actions to zoom in and out (pinch inward to zoom out and pinch outward to zoom in).

To select an item and open App Bar options for it on the Start screen, touch it and hold it for a second. This is the same motion if you are using touch in desktop programs where you also touch and hold the item; this will simulate a mouse right-click.

Using Windows 8.1 with a Keyboard and Mouse

If you are using Windows 8 with a keyboard and mouse, there are several time-saving shortcuts that you can use instead of touch gestures.

- *Right mouse click* or press *WindowsKey+Z* to display the App Bar in apps and at the Start screen
- Press *WindowsKey+C* to open the Charms Menu
- Press *WindowsKey+S* to open the Search charm

- Press *WindowsKey+Tab* to switch between running apps

You can also move your mouse to the four corners of the screen; these are called *hot corners*, and each will display different options. The top and bottom right corners will open the App Bar, and the top and bottom left corners will allow you to switch between running apps and opening the Start screen.

Using the On-Screen Keyboard

When you are using Windows 8.1 on a touchscreen, the on-screen keyboard will appear whenever you tap in a place where you would enter text, such as the address bar in Internet Explorer or a form on a website. When it appears, you will see the keyboard at the bottom of your screen, but if you're using your thumbs to type while holding your tablet in both hands, reaching the keys in the center of the keyboard can be tricky.

You can make the on-screen keyboard easier to use when you are holding your tablet in both hands by clicking the keyboard icon in the bottom right of the on-screen keyboard (Figure 1-9) to display different layout options, including:

- The standard on-screen keyboard
- A thumbs keyboard where the keys are moved to the far left and right of the screen
- Handwriting recognition, potentially useful if your tablet comes with a stylus
- Hiding the on-screen keyboard

Figure 1-9. The Windows 8.1 on-screen keyboard

You can select international characters on the on-screen keyboard by touching and holding a letter for one second. This will display accented letters that you can then touch to select.

Shutting Down and Restarting Windows 8.1

To restart or shut down Windows 8.1, follow these instructions.

- Open the Charms Menu
- Click/touch *Settings*
- In the panel that appears, click/touch *Power*
- In the menu that appears, click/touch *Shut Down*, *Restart*, or *Sleep* (Figure 1-10)

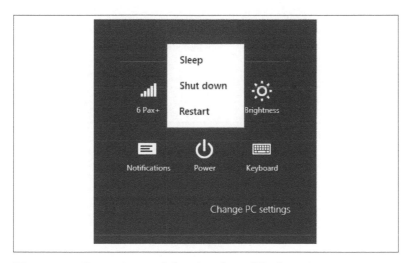

Figure 1-10. Restarting and shutting down Windows 8.1

Sleep puts your computer into a low-power *standby* state. This makes it very quick to switch on again, but it does consume a small amount of power, which can drain the battery on a laptop or tablet computer.

Summary

Windows 8.1 certainly offers a very new way of working, but it is simple and intuitive to use. In this chapter, I have shown you how to navigate the interface, launch apps, display menus, and move items to rearrange them, including arranging apps on your screen.

In Chapter 2, we will look at the things you will actually be doing with your computer, and I will show you how to connect to the Internet and check your email.

Using Email and the Internet

Whether you use a tablet, laptop, or desktop computer, you'll have it connected to the Internet. The Internet is now at the center of everything we do with our computers, from sending and receiving email to chatting and sharing photos and stories with friends and family. In Chapter 1, I showed you how to use the new interface in Windows 8.1. Now, let's see how you can get online and use the Internet Explorer web browser app and Windows 8.1's email app.

When you get a new computer, one of the very first things many people do is connect to the Internet to check email and catch up with friends and family. Windows 8.1 makes it very simple to get online, and all the tools you need are literally right at your fingertips.

Top Tips from This Chapter

1. If you sign into Windows 8.1 using the same login you use for your Hotmail or Live mail (this is called a Microsoft Account), many options in Windows 8.1 such as email, calendar, and the new Windows App Store will be automatically set up for you.

2. You can swipe left and right with your finger to automatically load the next and previous pages of a website in the Internet Explorer app.

3. The desktop version of Internet Explorer supports more features and allows you to organize many more Internet Favorites.

Getting Online with Windows 8.1

In your home, you will have an Internet router. This is the box that plugs into your phone line that provides Internet access for you. Some computers that remain static in the home, such as desktop PCs, can connect to these via a network cable–a physical cable connecting the computer to the router. This is usually the best way to get a stable and super-quick Internet connection. If you use WiFi to connect to your computer, place your router in a location where you will get a good signal throughout the building, and try to avoid putting it in a place where solid walls might block the signal.

Fixing WiFi Signal Problems

If you have a problem with the WiFi signal in your home, see if you can move your router to a better location, perhaps by using a telephone extension cable, or see if it is possible to install a *network cable* (that's all you need to ask for when purchasing one) that runs to the dead spots. Please note, though, that a cable does tie a computer to one location, some small laptops and tablets won't have a socket to plug the cable into, and trailing cables can also be a trip hazard.

If you connect a computer to your Internet router via a network cable, within a few seconds, you will have Internet access. If you don't, then try turning the router and PC off and on again.

Step by Step: Connecting to a Wireless Network

You will commonly want to connect your computer to the Internet via WiFi. You can also connect via a 3G or 4G (LTE) connection if your laptop or tablet supports it, and if you have either a SIM card installed in your computer, or a wireless broadband USB stick plugged in (Figure 2-1).

Figure 2-1. The WiFi and mobile broadband connection

1. Open the Charms by swiping in from the right of your screen with your finger or pressing *WindowsKey+C* on your keyboard.

2. Click/Touch the *Settings* Charm.

3. Click/Touch the *Network* icon, which is the first of six icons that will appear near the bottom right corner of your screen. It will say *Available* if Wireless Networks have been detected.

4. You will see Mobile Broadband (if your computer supports this) and WiFi networks listed separately. Click/Touch the name of the network to which you wish to connect.

5. You may be asked for a password; enter it here.

When you connect to a network, you will be asked if you want to find PCs, devices, and content on the network. This will include printers and shared files. Clicking this will allow you to open shared files but can also present opportunities where people on other PCs can see your files as well. Here's some guidance for what to click for different network types:

- *Home* networks should only be chosen when you are on your own WiFi network in your own home. This allows sharing of files, documents, and printers between computers. You can click *Yes* to this network type.

- *Work* networks allow certain sharing of files, documents, and printers, but they keep your own personal files safe from prying eyes. You can click *Yes* to this network type if you feel you trust the network.

- *Public* networks should always be selected if you are using WiFi in a coffee shop, on a train, or in another public location. This settings keeps your files, documents, and access to your computer safe and secure. You should always click *No* to this network type.

Additionally, any network where you do not need a password to get online is certainly insecure in that anybody can gain access to it. You should not allow the sharing of files on public networks or networks that are not protected by a password.

 If your WiFi connection isn't working, try restarting your router and perhaps your computer as well. If you connect to the Internet via a WiFi or Mobile broadband USB dongle, try unplugging it from the computer and plugging it into a *different* USB port. Also, do you have Airplane Mode switched on? You can check this at the top right of the screen when connecting to a network. Lastly, does your PC have a physical WiFi on/off switch that's accidentally been knocked?

Getting Quick Access to Your Email

Windows 8.1 comes with a new email app called Outlook, which you will see on the Start screen. Here you can easily send and receive emails using either a keyboard and mouse or the on-screen keyboard. If you log into your computer using the same Microsoft Account you use to access your Hotmail, MSN, or Live email account, then opening the *Outlook* app on the Start screen will automatically display your email.

If you use a different email provider, perhaps Gmail, you can add your email to the Mail app by following these instructions:

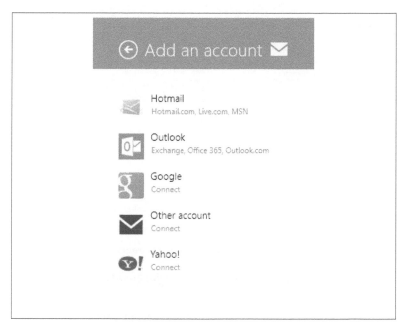

Figure 2-2. Connecting a new email account in the Outlook app

1. Open the *Outlook* app from the Start screen

2. Open the *Settings* Charm

3. In the top left of the screen click the *Accounts* link

4. Click the *Add an Account* link

5. You can now choose the type of account you want to add to Mail (Figure 2-2).

 You can also manage your email accounts by opening the Charms menu in the Outlook app and clicking/tapping the *Settings* icon. An *Accounts* link will then appear in the top right of the screen.

The Outlook app (Figure 2-3) has a **Power Pane** down the left side of the screen that includes quick links to…

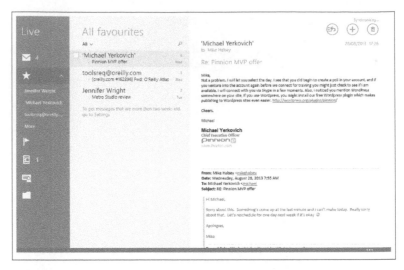

Figure 2-3. The Outlook app is a very powerful email client

- Your **Inbox**, click this to see your most recent email.
- Email from your **Favorite Contacts**, click this to open a list of people who have sent you email. You can click the *Star* button next to people to add or remove them from your favorites.
- **Flagged email**, you can click the *flag* icon next to an email to mark it for attention later.
- Email that's been classified by Outlook as **Newsletters**.
- Your **Contacts**, so you can send email to specific people and also see details of your contacts, including telephone numbers.
- A list of all your **Email Folders** that can be expanded.

The App Bar also includes innovative features such as being able to manage newsletters, junk, and spam email.

Using the Internet Explorer 11 App

Windows 8.1 comes with two copies of the Internet Explorer web browser, an easy to use app (Figure 2-4) and the desktop version you've probably used in earlier versions of Windows, I'll show you how to use this version later in this chapter, but for now we'll look at the app.

The address bar, where you type the addresses of the websites you want to visit, is at the bottom of the screen along with controls for *Back* (to the left of the address bar) to take you back a page and *Refresh* (to the right of the address bar) to reload the page. You can display these at any time by opening the App Bar.

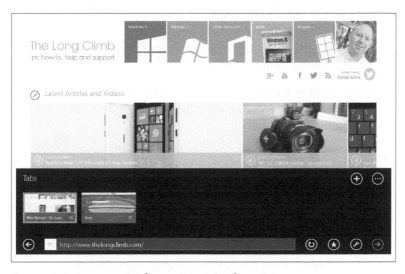

Figure 2-4. Internet Explorer 11 in Windows 8.1

Internet Explorer allows you to open multiple websites and switch between them using tabs. You can manage your tabs in Internet Explorer by opening the App Bar and you will see thumbnail images of your open tabs at the bottom of the screen.

You can also use touch gestures in Internet Explorer to move backward to previously loaded pages (*swipe left to right*) or to automatically move pages back and forth on a website (*swipe right to left*). This enables you to move through the pages of a website without needing to know what the next link is to click.

 There are many different options available in the Outlook app, and they can be accessed by opening the *Settings* charm and then clicking either *Accounts* and then clicking on your email account, or by clicking *Options* in the top right of your screen. These additional options include being able to download all of your email (the standard setting is just email from the last two weeks) and adding a signature to your email.

If you want to zoom in on part of a web page, or perhaps you are finding some text difficult to read or links too small to click or touch, the zoom feature can help. You can make a two-finger pinch zoom gesture on the screen to zoom in and out of any part of a web page in both the app and desktop versions of Internet Explorer. If you use a keyboard and mouse, you will need to use the desktop version of Internet Explorer to employ the zoom, and the zoom controls can be found in the bottom right corner of the window.

To open a new browser tab in Internet Explorer, click/touch or tap the + button to the right of the tabs when the App Bar is open and the tabs are showing.

 Windows 8 synchronizes your tabs between all your Windows 8.1 PCs. This means you can continue working on one PC with browser tabs you had open on another PC. To access your tabs from other PCs, click the *Tabs* link on the left of the App bar (next to your tabs) and the names of your other PCs will appear. Click a PC's name to see its open tabs.

So how do you get the best out of using Internet Explorer 11 in Windows 8.1? Here's a guide to how you can quickly perform the most common tasks from the App Bar.

- Click in the address bar, type a web address, and display your frequently visited websites.

- Click the *Favorites* button to display thumbnails of your saved Internet Favorites, a drop-down list (on the left) of your other Windows 8.1 PCs you can view tabs from and, on the right, *Add to Favorites* and *Pin to Start* buttons for the currently displayed web page.

- Click the *Tabs* button to display thumbnails for all your open tabs and, on the right, a button for opening a new tab and another button for opening an *InPrivate* tab and re-opening the most recently closed tab.

- Click the *wrench* button to display controls for finding text on the currently displayed web page, opening the web page in the desktop version of Internet Explorer, and viewing and files you have downloaded from the Internet.

Figure 2-5. Viewing recently visited and pinned websites in IE11

When you click/touch the address bar, Internet Explorer will show you the websites you have visited recently and also any Favorites that you have *pinned*. These pinned favorites are automatically displayed on the Start screen.

You can also save Internet Favorites by clicking the Favorites button on the App Bar and then clicking the *Add to Favorites* button. If you want to load one of these favorites later, open the App Bar and then click the Favorites button to display them (Figure 2-5). You can organize and arrange these into groups, and I will show you how to do this in more detail in Chapter 4.

 You can open the App Bar with your mouse in Internet Explorer by *right-clicking* in any blank space on a web page.

Saving Your Favorite Websites to the Start Screen

To save a favorite website to the Start screen or to create a quick link to it on the Start screen, which is called *pinning*, open the App Bar in

Internet Explorer and click/touch the *Favorites* button in the bottom right of the screen, then click either the *Add to Favorites* button or the *Pin* button. A pop-up panel will display details of the current website and will ask you to confirm that you want to save the current web page to your Favorites. If you pin websites to the Start screen you can later unpin them the same way you remove apps, and I will show you how to do this in Chapter 4.

Internet Explorer and Plug-Ins

A plug-in is a small program or toolbar that you can add to your web browser to expand its functionality. The app version of Internet Explorer does not support browser plug-ins and toolbars such as Adobe Acrobat Reader, but the Flash player, which is commonly used for playing video and games, is already built into the browser.

 Internet Explorer tells you if a website is known to be safe or unsafe by turning the address bar green or red. For shopping and banking websites, it will also display a padlock on the address bar if the website has adequate security. You should always look for a green address bar and/or the padlock when shopping or banking online.

Using InPrivate Mode

When you clean up your browser tabs in Internet Explorer, you will see a link to use InPrivate Mode. This is a special secure mode of Internet Explorer that prevents the browser from tracking where you have been, and also stops the website from placing any tracking files, known as cookies, on your computer.

InPrivate Mode is especially useful for birthdays and holidays when you're shopping for presents and surprises, and you don't want other people who use your computer to know what you're getting them.

Internet Explorer on the Desktop

Earlier, I mentioned Internet Explorer on the Windows 8.1 desktop. This version can add more flexibility than is available in the app version of Internet Explorer 11. You open Internet Explorer on the desktop by clicking or tapping the *Desktop* tile on the Start screen. You will then see Internet Explorer pinned to the Taskbar that runs along the bottom of the screen.

Unlike the app version of Internet Explorer, this desktop version supports browser plug-ins and toolbars and is also much better if you have a great many Internet favorites that you like to visit.

It works the same way as previous versions of Internet Explorer and other Internet browsers, and some users may prefer to use this version of the web browser.

 If you are viewing a web page in the Internet Explorer app, you can open it in the full desktop browser by clicking the *wrench* icon in the App Bar, then selecting *View on the Desktop* from the options that appear.

Using Outlook on the Desktop in Windows RT

If you have bought a tablet or ultrabook running the low power (long battery life) version of Windows 8.1 called **Windows RT**, such as a Microsoft Surface, you will in addition to the Outlook app also have some full Microsoft Office programs installed on the desktop (though you can't install more desktop programs in Windows RT). This includes the full version of the company's email and contacts software Outlook.

Figure 2-6. Setting up a new email account in Outlook

Outlook is Microsoft's full business email program. Indeed, if you use email at work you've probably been using Outlook for ages. It supports advanced features such as setting up appointments with other people, support for work email servers (commonly called Exchange servers), and it also includes built-in support for Skype calling and social networks such as Facebook and LinkedIn.

When you first start Outlook on the desktop in Windows RT (and these instructions are the same if you have purchased the full version of Microsoft Office for Windows 8.1) you will be asked if you want to set up an email account. The instructions are straightforward (Figure 2-6) and by just typing your name, email address, and password, Outlook is able to set up many different account types, including Gmail.

Figure 2-7. You can set up more email accounts and manage them later

You can also set up email accounts after this when running Outlook by clicking the *File* tab on the Ribbon and then clicking the *Account Settings* button (Figure 2-7). In Account Settings you can add, remove, and manage email accounts (perhaps to update a password).

 Outlook in Windows RT and Office 2013 has a special touch mode which can be activated by clicking the touch button (which looks like a hand with a pointing finger) in the very top left of the Outlook window.

Outlook on the desktop is controlled by a *Ribbon* interface, and these are the tabs you will see across the top of the window. They are...

- *File*, which contains the main program and email account options and settings
- *Home* has controls for creating new email, replying to or forwarding email, and setting up rules and categories for your email
- *Send/Receive* is where the button to manually check your email is to be found (the standard behavior of Outlook is to check for email every 30 minutes, though this can be changed in the Options, found under the *File* tab)

- *Folder* contains tools to help you organize and manage your email through the use of folders

- *View* contains controls for choosing how email is displayed in Outlook

Summary

It is very easy to get online with Windows 8.1, and if you use a Microsoft Account to sign into your computer, then Windows 8 takes all the strain out of setting up and configuring your email account, calendar, and more. Even if you use a Gmail, Yahoo!, or another account, it is quick and simple to set up your accounts in the People app.

If you want more control, the Windows Essentials Suite is an excellent package with some fantastic programs in it for blogging, photo editing, messaging, and more, and you can install it on desktop and laptop computers.

Now that you're online, in Chapter 3 I'll show you how you can share your files, photos, and more with friends and family, both inside your home and on the Internet.

Sharing Your Files, Photos, Music, and Video

Sharing our lives and experiences online is becoming ever more popular as digital cameras and smartphones are reduced in price and improved with every new model. Add to this social networking websites and instant messaging and it's easy to see why hundreds of millions of people are sharing things with friends and family online.

You might want to share files and memories with members of your own family and friends. Windows 8.1 is the most connected operating system Microsoft has ever produced, with features that are built in to make it simpler than ever to share files, photographs, music, and videos with family, friends, or the wider world through a blog or photo and video sharing website.

In Chapter 2, I showed you how to get online with Windows 8.1. Now let's look at how you can make sharing the best moments of your life enjoyable and problem-free.

Top Tips from This Chapter

1. Windows 8.1 includes features for sharing your files, photos, music, and videos, which you can access by clicking/touching *Share* in the Charms Menu.

2. You can share your files and even printers with other computers running Windows 8.1 or Windows 7 by setting up a HomeGroup.

3. You can share pictures, music, and video with non-Windows devices by turning on the Media Sharing feature in Windows 8.1.

The Windows 8.1 Sharing Tool

Windows 8.1 includes a new sharing tool that can be selected at any time from the *Charms*. If you are looking at a picture, file, video, or other type of content that you want to share with other people, click/touch *Share* and you will be shown a list of apps that you can share this content with instantly. This list will vary depending on what apps you have installed (Figure 3-1).

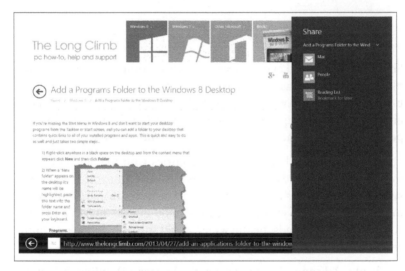

Figure 3-1. The Share Menu options in the Charms Menu

This is where the real power of social apps comes into play and where apps that you can download from the Windows Store can be much better and easier to use than visiting websites in Internet Explorer.

In Chapter 4, I will show you how to find and install apps in Windows 8.1, but for now, let me explain how Windows sharing works and why using apps can be better than visiting a website.

Let's say, for example, that you have photos that you want to share on Facebook or a video you want to upload to YouTube.

In earlier versions of Windows, you would open Internet Explorer or another web browser, go to the website, log in, and upload them. However, if you have a compatible app installed in Windows 8.1 for these websites—let's say, a YouTube app—you view the video you want to share, open the Charms, click/touch *Share*, and you will see the YouTube app appear in the list of compatible sharing apps.

Clicking/touching this app will automatically share the video with the app, and therefore on the website as well, with a minimum of fuss.

Sharing with Other People in Your Home

While Windows 8.1 makes it easy for you to share photos, videos, and more with friends and family on the Internet, it makes it just as easy to share things with people in your home on other computers. It does this using a *HomeGroup*.

You can find the settings for the HomeGroup by opening the *Settings* Charm and clicking *Change PC Settings*. The HomeGroup options are in the *Network* options (Figure 3-2).

Figure 3-2. HomeGroup options in Windows 8.1

Here, you will see switches making it easy to share *Documents, Music, Pictures,* and *Videos* from this computer. Each computer in a Home-Group can be configured differently so that, for example, a computer that's used in a home office might not share its Documents.

You can also share printers and other devices plugged into your computer. This makes it easy for people to be able to print documents or access other hardware (e.g., scanners or external hard disks) remotely, though the computer these are physically plugged into will need to be switched on.

 If you have a wireless printer, it can be accessed directly by other computers and won't need to be shared using Homegroup. I will show you how to set up printers in Chapter 7.

Sharing with Other Media Devices

Below the options for choosing what you want to share from your Windows 8.1 PC, you will see an option to *Allow all devices on the network such as TVs and game consoles to play my shared content*, but what does this mean?

Many devices in the home can now share content such as music and video even though they don't run Microsoft Windows. You might have a games console such as an Xbox or a PlayStation, an Internet-connected Smart TV, or an Internet radio. If you turn this option on, then all of these devices will be able to access your shared content—provided that they also have this feature enabled.

The advantage of this is that you can, for example, play your music library from your computer on your Internet radio in the garden, or watch videos you have stored on your computer on your living room TV.

Creating and Joining HomeGroups

Any computer running Windows 7 or Windows 8.1 can join a Home-Group. You can find the Homegroup options in PC Settings under the *Homegroup* section. You can create a HomeGroup by turning the feature on, and you will be shown a password that will need to be entered on other computers when they join the HomeGroup.

If a HomeGroup has already been created on another computer, you will see a *Join* button. Click/touch or tap this and you can click/touch or tap where you will be prompted to enter the HomeGroup password.

You can find this password in the HomeGroup settings on the computer the HomeGroup was created on.

If you no longer wish for a computer to be a member of a HomeGroup, you can also leave the HomeGroup by clicking/tapping the *Leave* button.

Connecting Windows 8.1 and Your Xbox

If you have an Xbox games console in your home, you can connect your Windows 8.1 computer to it. This gives you the advantage of being able to enjoy your music, photos, and videos on your TV.

Connecting to Your Xbox Using the Xbox SmartGlass App

You can connect your Windows 8.1 computer to your Xbox console through the *Xbox SmartGlass* app (Figure 3-3), which you can download for free from the Windows Store. I'll show you how to download and install apps in the next chapter.

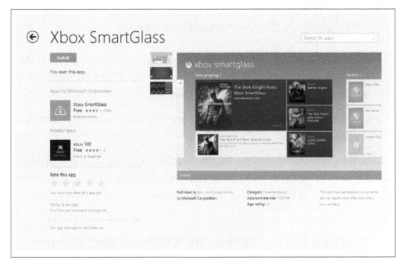

Figure 3-3. Downloading and installing the Xbox Companion App

The Xbox Companion app (Figure 3-4) allows you to control your Xbox console remotely from your Windows 8.1 computer. This includes being able to manage your Xbox Live account settings and games easily and using a Windows 8.1 tablet as a remote gaming control for the Xbox console.

Figure 3-4. Setting up the Xbox SmartGlass App

When you first start the Xbox SmartGlass, you will be asked to make your Xbox console available. You do this on the Xbox console itself from the Dashboard by opening the Xbox's *Settings*.

Changing this status setting will make sure that Windows 8.1 can detect the Xbox console.

To connect your Windows 8.1 PC to your Xbox console, you will need to be logged in to both the computer and the Xbox using the same Microsoft account (your Xbox Live account).

Connecting to Your Xbox Using Windows Media Center

When you connect your Xbox console to your computer using the Windows Media Center software on your desktop or laptop computer, you can share your pictures, music, and videos with the console and enjoy it on your TV.

To do this, you will need Windows Media Center installed on your computer. You can check by going to the All Apps view where, if Media Center is installed, it will appear in the *Windows Accessories* section. If you don't have Media Center installed, it is a chargeable extra that you can buy by searching for *Add Features* at the Start screen and selecting *Add Features to Windows 8* from the Settings search results.

You will need to buy an upgrade to Windows 8.1, which you can do by clicking the *I want to buy a product key online* button, which will upgrade you to the full version of Windows 8 Pro with Media Center (Figure 3-5).

To connect your Xbox 360 console to your Windows 8.1 PC using Windows Media Center, start Windows Media Center from the *Video* panel on your Xbox Dashboard and follow the simple instructions.

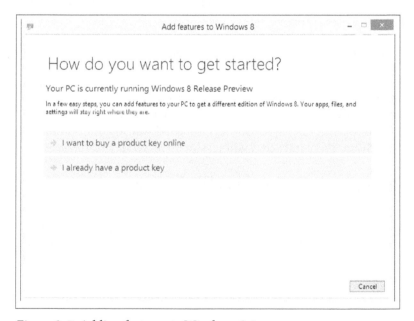

Figure 3-5. Adding features to Windows 8.1

If you do not have the full version of Windows 8 Pro with Media Center, you can share your pictures, music, and videos with an Xbox console by turning on the *Allow all devices on the network such as TVs and game consoles to play my shared content* setting in *HomeGroup* from PC Settings.

Connecting to Other Devices in Your Home

While you can use HomeGroup to share files and printers between other Windows 7 and Windows 8.1 computers in your home, and you can use the Xbox SmartGlass app or Windows Media Center to connect to an Xbox console, you can also connect your Windows 8.1 PC to other networked devices in your home. These could include a USB hard disk plugged into your Internet router or a wireless printer. There are a couple of ways that you can do this.

Connecting to Devices from the Charms

Open the Charms and select *Devices* to see other hardware devices you can use and access from your Windows 8.1 computer. Not all devices will appear in this view, so you may find that the specific device you want to use isn't displayed, but this is a good way to connect quickly to hardware that's fully compatible with Windows 8.1 features.

Connecting to Devices from File Explorer

To connect to other networked devices in your home, open *Desktop* from the Start screen and on the Taskbar that runs along the bottom of the desktop, click/touch the yellow folder icon to open *File Explorer*. Once File Explorer is open on your desktop, look in its left-hand panel, where you will see a link for *Network*.

Figure 3-6. Viewing network devices in Windows 8.1

Click/Touch this link to see all compatible network devices in your home. This will include other computers running Windows and any compatible computers such as Macs, networked media devices such as Internet radios, and any additional hardware such as a USB hard disk plugged into your Internet router if your router supports this feature (Figure 3-6).

You can access external hardware and computers directly from this panel to share files between them and your Windows 8.1 computer. Not all hardware devices will appear, however, and some that appear might not allow you to share files this way. For example, if you have a non-Windows 8.1 tablet such as an iPad or Android device, you will probably not be able to share files wirelessly. You might need to physically plug that tablet in to a desktop or laptop computer to copy files to it.

Summary

Sharing is becoming an ever more important and increasingly central part of our everyday lives. In Windows 8.1, it's easier than ever before to share your files, photos, music, and videos between Windows 8.1 apps and websites. If you have other hardware in your home that you want to share files with–perhaps to create a backup of your files–this is easy to do as well. I will show you how to create backups in Chapter 12.

I've mentioned already that some of the features I have talked about in this chapter require you to get apps from the Windows Store, and in Chapter 4, I'll show you how to use the Windows Store; how you can find, download, and install apps; and how you can manage them on your computer.

Downloading and Using Apps and Programs

To get the very best out of using your computer, you will want to install apps and programs. These can be anything from games to file and photo sharing and technical or financial apps, which are all now found in the Windows Store. You can access the *Store* from the Start screen.

It is the strength and variety of apps and programs that make Windows flexible and powerful and can allow people to use their computers for whatever tasks they wish, from entertainment to work.

While your Windows 8.1 computer comes with some great apps, including Outlook, Photos, Music, and News, you will probably want to install more apps and even programs that run on the Windows desktop, especially if you already have software from a previous PC that you want to use and that you are comfortable with at this time.

Windows 8.1 makes it easier than ever to find software with the new *Windows Store*, which can be launched from the Start screen. *All* Windows 8.1 apps can be found here; you can't get them anywhere else. Not only does this make apps simple to find, but it also makes the process of paying for them and downloading them much more secure because Microsoft scans all apps for malware.

Top Tips from This Chapter

1. The Windows Store is the central and safe place to find apps and programs.

2. You can drag and rearrange Tiles and icons on the Start screen to make them easier to find and organize.

3. You can view apps and desktop programs side by side, which can make working easier.

Using the Windows Store

You open the Windows Store by clicking the *Store* icon on the Start screen. It is arranged into app categories, including Games, Entertainment, and Books & Reference. There are also quick links for the most popular and highest-rated apps (Figure 4-1).

Figure 4-1. The Windows Store

You can find out more information on an app by clicking it. Here you will see the main information about the app in a panel on the left, and on the right, links to view the app's Overview, Details, and Reviews.

On the bottom under the screenshot images for the app, you will see a section called "This app has permission to use," where the Store will tell what personal information on your computer, if any, the app will want access to. Why is this important? Your personal information is of great economic value to companies. They want to know more about you so that they can directly target advertising at you and they may sell the information they hold about you to other companies.

If you allow an app access to information such as your email or Facebook account, you are potentially giving it huge volumes of very private information about you that you would otherwise not share. Always be careful in choosing apps, and do not install any that request access to information they should not ordinarily need.

Below this is an age rating for the app. This can be especially useful if you have young children who use your computer to play games.

You can install an app by clicking/touching the *Install* button, though you will have to register a credit or debit card with the Store to buy any apps that are not free.

At all stages while browsing apps, a *back* button will appear in the top left corner of your screen so you can return to the Store main page. You can also return to the main store page by clicking/touching *Home* from the App Bar.

 You can often find extra options and controls in an app by opening the Charms menu and clicking/tapping the *Settings* icon. If available in that app, extra options will appear in the top right of your screen.

Making Tiles Smaller and Larger

Some Tiles can be made larger and smaller, to display less or more information. You might want to make the Outlook tile smaller, for example, so that it only shows you the number of new emails and not the senders and subjects (if perhaps other people can read over your shoulder), or you may have a news Tile that when made larger shows you additional information about current events (you can see an example of the four different sizes of Tile in Figure 4-2).

Figure 4-2. Different sized tiles

You can make a Tile larger or smaller by *touching and holding it* with your finger or *right-clicking* it with your mouse. From the App Bar, you can then click/touch the *Resize* button. If you do not see a Resize option, then the tile you have selected cannot be resized.

You can also turn the Live Tile aspect of the app off completely, perhaps for privacy reasons, by selecting *Turn Live Tile Off* from the App Bar when you have selected it. This prevents the Tile from displaying information such as details of emails, photos, or calendar appointments.

Organizing App Icons on the Start Screen

When you install new apps on your Windows 8.1 computer they don't appear in your Start screen straight away, you will need to pin them there. This is because your Start screen could become cluttered quite quickly if apps auto-pinned themselves, making it very difficult to find what you are looking for. As you add Tiles to the Start screen, it expands to the right and can get very large.

You can pin tiles to the Start screen by opening the All Apps view. This is opened with touch by swiping upward on the Start screen. With your mouse you will see a small down arrow near the bottom left of the screen. Click this to open the All Apps view.

You pin an app (or multiple apps simultaneously) by right-clicking them (touching and holding with touch) and from the App Bar clicking the *Pin to Start* button. You can also move Tiles around the Start screen to organize them, and hide them back to the All Apps view to help keep them organized.

You open the All Apps view by swiping upward on the Start screen with your finger or by clicking the small down arrow with your mouse that appears near the bottom left of the screen.

If you are using a mouse, remember to look for the scroll bar at the bottom of your screen. You can drag this to move left and right on the Start screen. You can also use your mouse scroll wheel to pan left and right on the Start screen.

You might want to reorganize the tiles on your Start screen so that all the apps, websites, and programs you use regularly have their Tiles on the far left of your screen, to make them easier to access. You might also install software such as Microsoft Office and want to hide the extra programs it installs, such as the Office Picture Viewer.

Arranging the Start Screen Step by Step

To arrange your apps, websites, and programs on the Start screen (see Figure 4-3), follow these quick steps:

- Click/Touch and then hold, drag, and drop tiles around the Start screen to rearrange them using either your finger or your mouse.

- Hold a tile between groups to create a new group again using either your finger or your mouse. Drop it on the vertical bar that appears.

- Remove a tile from the Start screen by touching and holding it, or *right-clicking* with your mouse, and then click/touch *Unpin from Start* from the App Bar.

To leave the customize view click or touch anywhere in a blank space on the Start screen or press the *Esc* key on your keyboard.

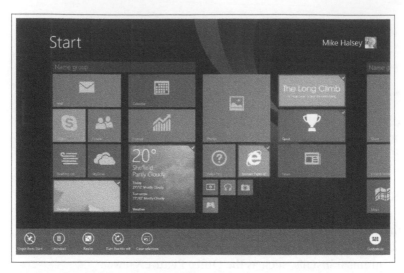

Figure 4-3. Working with Live Tiles

If you unpin a Tile from the Start screen, it will be removed, but you will still be able to access it when you want to. I will show you how to do this later in this chapter. You will notice that in the *Customize* view (which can also be accessed by clicking the *Customize* button of the Start screen App Bar) you can also name groups of tiles. You might, for example want to name then "Work," "Internet," and "Games." This can help you identify your groups of apps.

Arranging Groups of Tiles

I mentioned previously that you can create new groups of Tiles by dragging a Tile to the space between groups and, when you see a vertical bar appear, dropping the Tile. You can also name and rearrange whole groups of Tiles simply and quickly.

You can give groups of Tiles names by zooming out of the Start screen (see Figure 4-4). You can do this in one of three ways:

- Make an outward pinch zoom gesture with your fingers
- *Click* with your mouse in the very bottom right corner of the Start screen
- Hold the *Ctrl* key on your keyboard and use your mouse wheel to zoom out

You can now drag and rearrange whole groups of tiles to arrange them however best suits you.

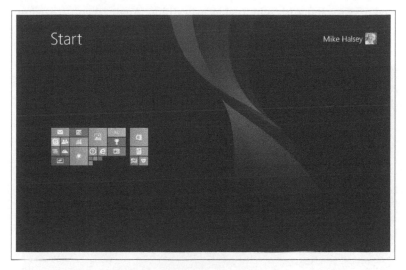

Figure 4-4. Zooming out of the Start screen

Viewing All Your Installed Apps and Programs

I showed you earlier how you can hide apps and programs from your Start screen. But surely if you hide them, then you can't use them? Fortunately, it's easy to see all of the apps and programs that you have installed on your computer at any time.

To see hidden apps and programs, open the App Bar from the Start screen and click/touch the small down arrow that appears in the bottom left of the Start screen or swipe upward with your finger. Here, you will be able to see all the apps and programs that are installed on your computer (Figure 4-5). Programs are organized into groups as you would see in the Start Menu in previous versions of Windows.

You cannot rearrange apps and programs in the All Apps view into different groups, but it is easy to see all the software you have installed and you can view them in different ways. In the top left of the All Apps view you will see a *by name* link. You can click this to view your apps and programs in different ways, such as *by category*, *by date installed*, or *most used*.

In the top right of the All Apps view is a search box you can use to find an app or program if you're having difficulty finding it in the list. Remember, this view can also expand outward to the right, so you may need to swipe left and right to view everything. Again, if you are using a mouse, a scroll bar will appear at the bottom of the screen.

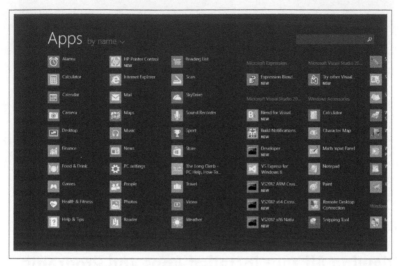

Figure 4-5. The All Apps view

Don't Have Too Much Software Installed

Sometimes it's easy to have lots of apps and programs installed on your Windows 8.1 computer. Perhaps you have downloaded apps to try them, and you later decide you don't want to use them.

You should always keep the number of apps and programs on your computer to a minimum. Having too much software installed can cause Windows 8.1 to slow down over time, and it can also make it much more difficult to find the app or program you want to use.

I would also recommend against installing any app or program that duplicates a function that is already part of Windows; for example, CD or DVD burning software, mapping software, or another web browser. Each extra piece of software adds to the overall complexity of the computer, and with complexity can come instability, as I write about in my book *Troubleshoot and Optimize Windows 8 Inside Out* (Microsoft Press).

Switching Between Running Apps and Programs

Apps in Windows 8.1 run full screen by default, but you will want to switch between them and use more than one at a time. There are several different ways to switch between running apps and programs on your computer. If you are using touch, then dragging your finger in from the left of your screen will drag the previously seen app onto the screen.

You can also display a list of the currently running apps by swiping in from the left of your screen with your finger and then, in the same movement, swiping back out again.

 You can shut down any running app by dragging it off the bottom of the screen. This includes app thumbnails and the currently running app.

With your keyboard, you can use the *WindowsKey+Tab* keypress to switch between running apps or the *Alt+Tab* key combination to switch between all running app and desktop programs. The WindowsKey is in the bottom right of your keyboard, with the Windows logo on it, and Tab can be found near the top left of the keyboard.

To switch between apps using the keyboard, hold down the Alt or Windows Key and keep pressing Tab until you get to the program you want. The currently running apps and programs will appear as thumbnail images at either the left side of the screen or in the center of the screen.

Viewing Apps Side by Side

You can also view apps (and even the desktop) side by side on your screen. To view apps side by side, grab the app at the top of the screen with your finger or mouse and drag it toward the center of the screen. You will see that it changes to a thumbnail image. When you drag this thumbnail to the left or right of the screen, you will see a vertical bar appear; this signifies that dropping the app there will dock it in a panel to that side of the window. You can now return to the Start screen and run another app. This second app will appear, filling the main portion of the screen with your *docked* app sitting at the left or right of it.

If your screen has sufficiently high resolution (normally HD) you can have three or even four apps running side by side. With two apps running, return to the Start screen and start another app. This new app will then appear as a thumbnail image between the currently running apps on your screen (Figure 4-6). You can drag this app left or right to replace the apps that are on that side of the screen, or you can hold the app between them. If a gap opens up you can drop the app there to display all the apps together.

Figure 4-6. Viewing two apps side by side

 You can also select another running app by holding down the *WindowsKey* on your keyboard and pressing the *Tab* key to cycle through thumbnail images of running apps. For desktop programs, use the key combination *Shift+Tab* instead.

When you have two or more apps running on your screen you can change their sizes by dragging the bar that separates them to the left and right. You can also drag this bar to the far edge of the screen to remove an unwanted app from view completely.

Viewing Two Desktop Windows Side by Side

You can also view desktop programs side by side (Figure 4-7). This can be very useful for comparing two documents or web pages. To do this, click/touch or touch and hold the top of the desktop program window and drag it to the far left or right of your screen. You will see a shadow appear when your mouse touches the screen edge to show you that the program will be resized to fill exactly half of your screen's width and docked to one side of the screen.

Drag your other program to the opposite side of the screen and it will fill the other half of your screen's width. You can return them to their original shape and size by dragging them away from the side of the screen in the same way that you put them there.

Figure 4-7. Viewing two desktop programs side by side

To compare two web pages side by side when you have multiple tabs open in the desktop version of Internet Explorer, drag an individual tab out of the window and it will then appear in its own Internet Explorer window. These can then be snapped to the left and right of the screen.

Uninstalling Apps and Programs in Windows 8.1

You won't always want to have every app or program installed forever. You may, for example, have installed something just to try it out or because you thought it was what you were looking for, only to discover later that it is an app or program you don't want to keep.

You can uninstall any app or program from the Start screen or the All Apps view by *touching and holding it* or *right-clicking* on it. In the App Bar, you will see an uninstall option.

If you are uninstalling a desktop program, you will be taken to the *Programs and Features* window on the desktop. Here, you should click the program you wish to uninstall and on the toolbar near the top of the window, you will see an option to uninstall the program.

Summary

There are many cool ways to work with apps and programs in Windows 8.1, and the Windows Store will help keep malware off your computer as well as making it much simpler to find the software you want. Security is still important, though, and I will show you how to keep your computer safe in Chapter 11.

It's well worth spending some time arranging your apps and programs into groups on the Start screen, because this will make it much easier to find things later on.

Now that I've shown you how to use and work with apps and programs in Windows 8.1, in Chapter 5, I'll show you how you can enjoy playing your music and videos.

Watching and Listening to Your Videos and Music

As you accumulate your collections of digital music and videos, you'll want to enjoy this content on your Windows 8.1 computer. Windows 8.1 comes with some excellent apps that make it easy to enjoy and organize your media.

Top Tips from This Chapter

1. Windows 8.1 comes with apps for playing both music and videos.

2. When looking at links in apps that have a down arrow to their right, you can click/touch the arrow for more options.

3. If you have a desktop computer, a laptop, or a Windows 8.1 Pro tablet, you can also use Windows Media Player to sort, organize, and play your music and video collection.

Watching Your Videos in Windows 8.1

You can play your videos in the *Videos* app, which you can access from the Start screen. When you first open the Videos App, you will be presented with a display showing videos that you can watch or purchase online (Figure 5-1).

Figure 5-1. The Videos app

To view your own videos, you should pan left either with a swipe of your finger or by moving your mouse to the bottom of the screen, where you will find the scroll bar. You can also use the scroll wheel on your mouse to move around left and right in Apps.

Your video display will show you your most recently added videos. To view all of your videos, click/touch the *My Videos* link at the top of this section.

 Click or tap the back arrow in the top left of the screen at any time to return to the previous page.

There are several different ways to organize your videos. Near the top left of the screen, you can click/touch on the *Date Added* link to view your video library in different ways, such as *A to Z* or by *duration*. You can click/touch on any video to play it, and you will see play controls appear on the screen, which will fade when you don't touch the screen or move the mouse for a few seconds, but they will reappear when you do touch the screen or move the mouse.

At any time, you can *right-click* with your mouse or swipe upward with your finger from the bottom of the screen to open more controls on the App Bar.

You may have videos stored in different folders on your computer or perhaps in a different location, such as an external USB hard disk. To play files in different locations, open the App Bar and click/touch *Open File*. This will open the folder view where you can look through all your files and folders to view any videos (Figure 5-2). This also applies to the Music App in Windows 8.1.

Figure 5-2. The Folder view

Using the Folder View

The *Open File* view allows you to view any files you have stored, not just on your own computer, but also in compatible Internet services such as Microsoft SkyDrive on your home network and, if you have a Windows Phone and use the *Windows Phone* app to connect to your PC, you can also access video you have recorded on the phone as well. You can click/touch on any link that has a view. For example, clicking the *Files* link will display folders, including your documents, pictures, and even your entire computer and network. Below this are links to other available locations, such as SkyDrive.

You move around folders in this view by clicking on them. If you want to move up a folder location, click/touch the *Go Up* link. Videos can be opened and played by clicking or touching them.

Playing Your Music in Windows 8.1

The Music app is also opened from the Start screen and looks and works in a very similar way to the Video app. When you first open it, you are shown music that you can purchase online. Swipe left to view your own music collection (or move your mouse to the bottom of the screen and a scroll bar will appear that you can drag left).

The Music app will show your most recently added music first. Click/ touch the *My Music* link to view the whole music collection on your computer. Here you can arrange your music by *Songs*, *Albums*, or *Artists* by clicking the links on the left side of the screen (Figure 5-3). You can also view any *Playlists* you have created. More on creating playlists will follow shortly.

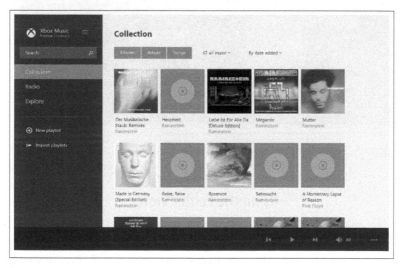

Figure 5-3. Viewing your music collection

 You can create a new playlist at any time in the Music app by clicking/touching the + *New playlist* button on the left of the screen.

You can click/touch the *Date Added* link at the top of the screen to sort and arrange your music in different ways, including by *genre* or by *A to Z*.

When you click/touch on an album, the screen changes to display a track list for that album (Figure 5-4). Here, you can click/touch on an individual track to play. *Play, add to playlist, artist details*, and *more options* buttons appear top center above the track list, and in the bottom right of the screen are *next (and previous) track, play*, and *volume* controls.

At any time when music is playing, you can also click/touch the + button next to the name of the currently playing track to add the track to the end of the current music playlist.

Figure 5-4. Playing music

 Open the App Bar at any time to display the play controls in the Music and Video apps.

Using Windows Media Player

If you want more control over your music library and you are using a desktop computer, laptop, or Windows 8.1 Pro tablet, you can use

Windows Media Player (Figure 5-5). You can start Windows Media Player by searching for *media* at the Start screen.

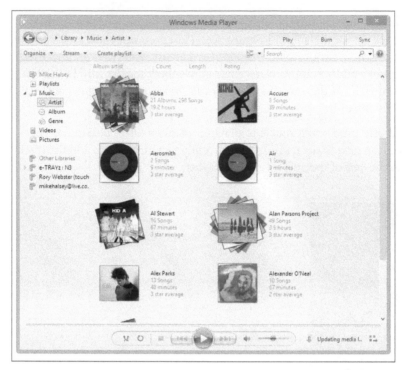

Figure 5-5. Windows Media Player

This software offers several advantages over the Music app, especially for people with large music collections. In the left panel are quick links to let you arrange and view your music by *Artist, Album,* or *Genre,* and you can also view your *Videos* and *Pictures* here as well. Below these links are direct links to any other computers or network devices that are sharing pictures, music, and video on your network. This can include other computers and network storage.

Perhaps the best functionality with Windows Media Player is the advanced ability to control playlists. Click/Touch *Create Playlist* in the options bar that runs along the top of the window and you can create either a standard playlist or an auto playlist. Let me explain the difference.

When you create a Standard playlist, it will appear in the left-side navigation panel in Windows Media Player. You can drag and drop music onto this playlist using your mouse to add music to it.

Auto playlists, however, will automatically add music to the playlists depending on various criteria that you set (Figure 5-6). You can choose from a great many options here to create, for example, auto playlists of your most played music or even music tracks that you've never played.

Figure 5-6. Windows Media Player

If, at any time, you want to create an audio CD—perhaps to play your favorite music in the car—you can do this by clicking the *Burn* link in the top right of the window and dragging and dropping the music tracks you want into the panel that appears. When you have selected the tracks you want, click/touch the *Start Burn* button to burn your audio CD (you will need a blank CD and a CD burner drive in your computer to do this).

Summary

The built-in apps for playing music and videos in Windows 8.1 are perfectly capable, although you might prefer to use an alternative player such as the excellent Zune Desktop software from Microsoft or, if you have an iPhone, iTunes software. If you are using a Windows 8.1 tablet, you won't be able to install these desktop software packages, but alternative music and video playing apps will be available in the Windows Store. See Chapter 4 for details of how to install apps and software.

In Chapter 6, I'll show you how you can view your pictures and photographs on your computer, how you can import images from a digital camera, how you can do basic editing on your photos, and then how to display them as slideshows.

Importing, Viewing, and Editing Your Photographs and Videos

Photographs are an ever-important part of life, allowing us to relive precious moments or share in the experiences of our friends and family. Digital cameras have allowed us to take many more photographs than we could have with film cameras and to share them in new and exciting ways both with friends and family and also with the wider world. You can read more about how to share your digital photographs in Chapter 3.

While your digital camera will probably come with software that will enable you to import photos and organize them in different ways, Windows 8.1 includes many of these features as standard so that in many cases there's no need to install the additional software that came with your camera.

Top Tips from This Chapter

1. Windows Photo Gallery, free from Microsoft, includes some excellent photo-management and editing tools.

2. You can choose what happens when you plug a memory card into your computer through the *Default Programs* panel.

3. Tags can be added to photos to make them easier to find.

Importing Photos and Video from Your Digital Camera

You can import photos and video from your digital camera or camcorder in the same way, either by plugging your camera directly into your computer using a cable, or by removing the memory card from the camera and inserting it into a card reader built into or attached to the PC.

 If you plug a high-capacity memory card (32GB or above in size) into your PC and all that happens is the PC says it's unformatted, your card reader might be an older model that's unable to read the newer, higher-capacity memory cards, try plugging your camera into your PC via USB instead.

When you insert your memory card into your PC or plug your camera in via a USB or other cable, you will be taken to the Photos app import screen (Figure 6-1). Here you will be shown thumbnail images of all the photos on your memory card and all the pictures and videos that are new (at least that have not previously been marked on the memory card as having been imported already) will be selected.

 You can bulk select photos by clicking the first in a group to be imported and then holding down the *Shift* key on your keyboard when you click the last one in the group.

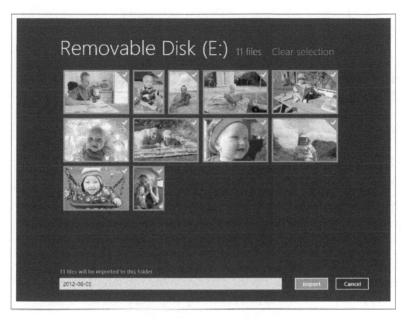

Figure 6-1. The Photo and Video Import Wizard

You can select which photos and videos on the camera or memory card you want to import by clicking them. By default, it will create a folder in your *Pictures* library named for the date (year, month, day) you have imported the photos, but you can rename the file. To change the name of the folder your photos and video will be imported to, perhaps from *2012-06-14* to *Amsterdam, October 2012*, click/touch the white box at the bottom of the screen to edit the folder name.

 If not all of your photos and videos are appearing on the screen, scroll to the right to view more of them, as only so many will be displayed on the screen at one time.

When you are ready to import photos and videos to your computer, click/touch the *Import* button in the bottom right of the screen to start the import process. When this is complete, you will be asked if you want to open the album you have created to view the imported photos and videos on your computer.

The imported photos will not be deleted from your memory card or camera during this import process, so you will have to delete them afterward, either using File Explorer on the Windows 8.1 desktop or the camera settings.

Advanced Photo and Video Import Using Windows Photo Gallery

Sometimes you want more control over your photos—certainly when it comes to editing them—and this is where Microsoft's Windows Photo Gallery software is useful. You can download it as part of the Windows Essentials Suite (*http://download.live.com*).

With Windows Photo Gallery installed on your Windows 8.1 computer (it won't install on a Windows RT tablet), you get much more control over the photo and video import process.

To import photos using Windows Photo Gallery, open the Photo Gallery software and click/tap the *File* tab in the top left of the window. From the options that appear, click/tap *Import photos and videos*.

 If you are automatically taken to the Windows 8.1 Photo and Video Importer app, search for *Default* at the Start screen and run the *Default Programs* option that appears. Click/Touch *Change autoplay settings* in the page that appears and change the *Camera Storage* option to either *Import Photos and Videos (Windows Photo Gallery)* or *Ask me every time*.

A new import window will now appear where you have more choices. Let's look at each of these in turn (Figure 6-2).

 If the photo and video import options aren't appearing when you plug your camera or memory card into your computer, open the *Photos* app and from the App Bar select *Import*. Here, you will be able to tell Windows 8.1 where to import your pictures from.

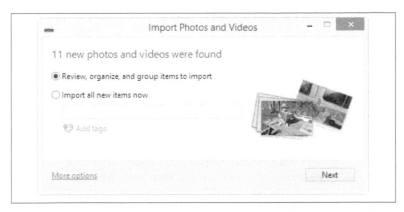

Figure 6-2. The Photo and Video Import Wizard (Windows Photo Gallery)

Review, Organize, and Group Items to Import

This option will group your photos by the date they were taken. This allows you to split photos taken on a longer trip or vacation into different folders to keep them separate. At the top of each group, as you can see in Figure 6-3, you can enter a name for that group. Let's say you were on a European road trip. On the first day you were in the Netherlands; on the second and third days, you were in Germany; and on the fourth day, you visited Poland. Because the Import Wizard splits the photos into groups sorted by date, you can label each group of photos appropriately.

If the photo groups are not appearing correctly, you can use the *Adjust groups* slider in the bottom right of the window to create more or fewer groups, again arranged by date and time.

You can also select which photos and videos you wish to import by checking and unchecking the boxes in the top left of each thumbnail image. There are three different types of box you can check.

1. The *Select all* check box will select every photo and video for import.

2. You can check the box to the left of each group to select all of the items in that group.

3. You can select photos and videos individually using the check box to left of its thumbnail image.

What is a tag?

A tag is a keyword that describes the content of a picture. For example if a photo was taken with your family in Egypt, you might use the tags *family*, *egypt*, and *holiday*. If a photo was taken with Phil at the rodeo, you can use the tags *Phil* and *rodeo*. When you are searching for photos, you can use these tags to make the search easier, for example searching for *rodeo* will display all the photos taken at rodeos and tagged with that keyword, regardless of what rodeo they were at and when they were taken.

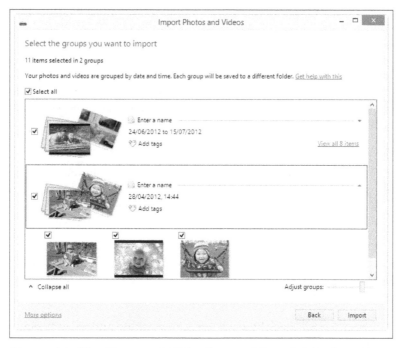

Figure 6-3. The Photo and Video Import Wizard (Windows Photo Gallery)

In the bottom left of the import window is a *More options* link. This provides additional functionality, such as choosing the default import folder location for pictures and videos, the default naming convention for new photos and videos, whether you want Windows Photo Gallery to automatically rotate images so they are correctly oriented, and if you want photos and videos to be automatically deleted from your camera or memory card on import to Windows.

Import All New Items Now

The second option at the main import screen is much more straightforward. It will import every photo and video from the camera or memory card. You will be prompted to give a name for the photos, perhaps *Dusseldorf, October 2013*, and this will be the name of the folder, and each imported photo and video will be labelled according to this name.

Additionally, you can click/touch the *Add tags* link to add key words to the photos and videos that can make them easier to search for and organize. For example, you might add the words *holiday* and *Germany*. You can then search for *Germany* in Windows Photo Gallery, the Photos app, or File Explorer to bring up all photos taken in that country. You should separate all individual tags with a semicolon (;).

Viewing Your Photos in Windows 8.1

The *Photos* app, accessible from the Start screen, is the main location for viewing your digital photo collection (Figure 6-4). This app allows you to view all the photos you have stored on your PC. The app also includes basic photo editing, accessible through the App Bar. At any time, you can move back a folder by clicking the back arrow in the top left of the screen.

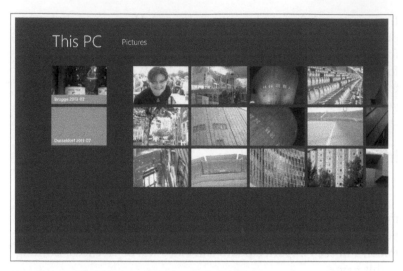

Figure 6-4. The Photos app in Windows 8.1

The editing controls (Figure 6-5), accessed by clicking *Edit* on the App Bar, include the controls you will use most often to correct or touch-up a photo. These tools include rotating, cropping, fixing red-eye, adjusting the brightness and contrast, color temperature, and tint. There is also a selection of effects you can apply to a photo.

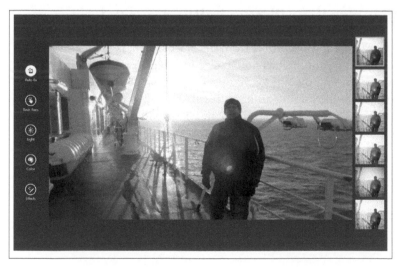

Figure 6-5. The Photos app includes basic photo editing

You can cancel photo editing by opening the App Bar and clicking the *Cancel* button

 If you want to share one or more photos by email or on the Internet, select them by either *right-clicking* each one with your mouse or by *tapping and pulling downward* with your finger. Alternatively, you can open the App Bar and click/touch the *Select All* button. You can now open the Charms menu and click/touch *Share*. A list of compatible apps you can use to share your photos will appear; tap the appropriate app to share the photos.

Editing Your Photos in Windows Photo Gallery

The Photos app in Windows 8.1 doesn't support editing your photos, and it's well worth looking through the Microsoft Store to find photo-editing apps that you can use (Figure 6-6). If you see Adobe Photoshop Touch available, this is always an excellent purchase.

However, if you have downloaded the Windows Essentials Suite, Windows Photo Gallery offers some easy to use and really quite powerful photo-editing tools. You can double-click/touch a picture to open it in editing mode, and you will see that the Ribbon at the top of the window changes to an *Edit* tab. There are many controls to choose from, but I want to detail the ones you are most likely to use.

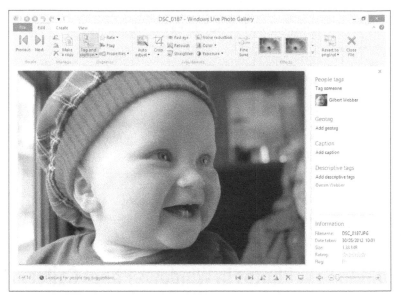

Figure 6-6. Windows Photo Gallery

- The *Manage* section includes controls for rotating the image.
- The *Organize* section allows you to add and manage tags. These can be used to make it easier to search for specific images.
- The *Adjustments* panel is where the editing tools can be found.
- *Auto adjust* will attempt to intelligently edit the brightness, contrast, rotation, and other aspects of the photograph.
- *Crop* allows you to trim the image down to a smaller size, removing unwanted items from the main focus of the picture.
- *Red eye* will help remove the red eye effect caused by some cameras. You can click/touch on the red in people's eyes to have it intelligently removed.
- *Fine Tune* gives you more control over the adjustments made by the *Auto adjust* feature.
- *Revert to Original* is a very useful feature if you have made changes to a picture that you did not intend to make or that changed the photo in an unwelcome way. When you edit a photo using Windows Photo Gallery, a backup of the original image is made automatically. At any time, you can click/touch the *Revert to Origi-*

nal button to restore that original image and undo any changes you have made.

Using Your Lock Screen as a Digital Photo Frame

You can use the Lock screen on your Windows 8 PC as a digital photo frame. This can be useful if you have a Windows tablet such as a Surface, which comes with a stand. You can use any (or indeed all) of the pictures on your PC to display and you configure it through PC Settings.

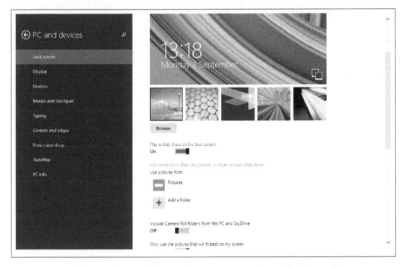

Figure 6-7. You can use the Lock screen as a digital photo frame

To turn the Lock screen into a digital photo frame, click the *Settings* charm and then click *Change PC Settings* in the bottom right of the screen. When PC Settings open, click the tile for the *Lock screen* at the top of your screen.

When the Lock screen settings open, in the *Slide Show* section you will see your Pictures folder is selected, but you can click/touch this to remove it and add a different, or several different, pictures folders to use as the Slide Show.

Below these options are two additional switches. The first controls how long your PC is inactive before it locks and displays the Slide

Show. This can be from 1 minute to 1 hour. The second switch tells the PC to switch off the display when the slide show has been running for a certain period of time, or not to turn off at all. Remember though that unless your PC is plugged in, leaving the Slide Show running will drain the battery.

When you are ready to activate the Slide Show and use your Lock screen as a digital photo frame, click/tap the Slide Show *On* switch.

Summary

Our photographs are precious, and we want to be able to enjoy and preserve them. Windows 8.1 includes some excellent features that enable us to import photos from digital cameras and also to share your digital photographs with friends and family.

In the next chapter I'll show you how to change the look and feel of Windows 8.1 and how you can make the operating system easier to see, use, and hear.

Personalizing your Windows 8.1 Experience

Windows has always been the most customizable and configurable operating system available, and with Windows 8.1 there is no change. You can change everything from the colors on the Start screen and desktop to the PC's sounds and more. You can also adjust these options to make Windows 8.1 easier to see, use, and hear. In this chapter I will show you how to set up Windows 8.1 just as you want it.

Top Tips from this Chapter

1. The Ease of Access features can make Windows 8.1 much easier to see, use, and hear

2. You can set the desktop wallpaper to be the background for your Start screen

3. You can start Windows 8.1 directly to the desktop and customize the All Apps view to show your desktop programs first

Personalizing the Start screen

In Chapter 4 I showed you how to arrange tiles on the Start screen, adding and removing them and arranging them into groups. You can also customize the Start screen itself through the *Settings* charm. When you open this from the Start screen you will see a *Personalization* link appear in the top right of your screen (Figure 7-1).

Figure 7-1. You access the Personalization options from the Settings charm

The Personalization panel is separated into three sections, (Figure 7-2). The top section contains different background images that can be used on your Start screen. In Windows 8.1 some of these images are animated, and the last two available in the list will always be a blank background and your desktop wallpaper.

Next is the color of the Start screen background. You will see there are many colors available at the bottom of this section on a slider. When you choose a color on this slider, a series of 18 shades for that color will appear in the main box above it.

This works the same for the accent color, the bottom section in the panel. The accent is not just the main shade for the pattern on the background but it is also the accent for buttons, switches, the App Bar, and notification text on the Start screen, PC Settings, and in app settings and menus.

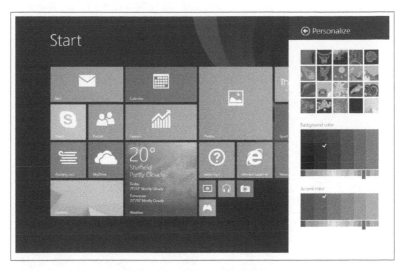

Figure 7-2. You can choose background and accent colors for personalization

 Some background colors, most notably in PC Settings, are always a light, pale color. With this in
mind you should choose an accent color that is
legible against a lighter background.

Personalizing the Desktop

You can also personalize many options on the desktop as with previous
versions of Windows. There are two ways to access the desktop personalization options on the desktop. You can select *Personalization*
from the top right of your screen after opening the *Settings* charm, or
you can right-click in any blank space on your screen to display a
Personalization option.

The main *Personalization* options display a series of themes that you
can choose from (Figure 7-3). Some include a single wallpaper, and
others include multiple wallpapers that the desktop will cycle through
on a specified schedule. You can click or tap any theme to activate it.

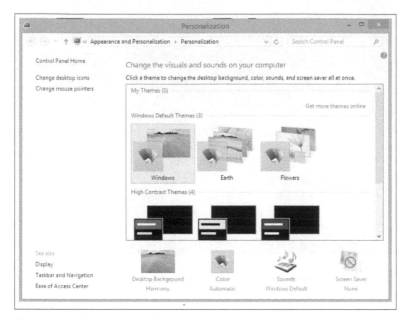

Figure 7-3. The desktop also offers personalization options

At the bottom of the desktop Personalization window are four options...

- **Desktop Background** allows you to set one or multiple images as your desktop background (Figure 7-4). To select multiple images with your keyboard and mouse, hold down the *Ctrl* key when you click each one. At the bottom of the window is a picture position option and, if you have selected multiple images for the desktop, a *Change picture every...* option where you can set how often the desktop background will change.

Figure 7-4. You can cycle the desktop between multiple backgrounds

If you set multiple desktop wallpapers and then also set the Start screen to use your desktop background, that Start screen background will also cycle through the selected wallpapers.

- **Color** is where you can set the color for your desktop windows (Figure 7-5). This can be a fixed color or, if you click the color swatch option, the desktop windows will change color to match and compliment the desktop background wallpaper.

Figure 7-5. You can set the color of desktop windows

- **Sounds** is where you can change the default sounds that Windows 8.1 makes, for example the startup and shutdown sounds.

- **Screen saver** should *only* be used if you are still using an older Cathode Ray Tube (CRT) monitor with your PC and not a flat panel screen. Screen savers help avoid CRT monitors from having images physically burned onto the screen when left for long periods of time. If you use a flat panel display with your PC this can't happen and you will use much less electricity by having the screen turn off after a period of time instead, which is the standard setting.

Making Things on Your Screen Larger or Smaller

Sometimes you will want to make things on your screen larger and easier to read. This is less of a problem on the Start screen and in apps as it is on the desktop where text and window controls can often be very small, especially on tablets and ultrabooks.

Fortunately you can scale everything up on your screen without making anything blurry. To do this, *right-click* or tap and hold anywhere in a blank space on the desktop and from the menu that appears click *Screen Resolution*. The window that appears will allow you to change the screen resolution. This was traditionally the way to scale up a display but while it works on CRT monitors, on a flat panel screen it will just make everything blurry and fuzzy.

Instead click the *Make text and other items larger or smaller*, link and you will see a slider (Figure 7-6) that will allow you to scale everything on the desktop. Scaling things upward can make buttons and menu options much easier to read and also to use with touch (useful on a Windows 8.1 or Windows RT tablet).

Figure 7-6. You can make items on the desktop smaller or larger

Making Windows 8.1 Easier to Use

In addition to making things on the Windows desktop larger and easier to see and poke with your finger, you can activate a full gamut of accessibility options that can help make Windows 8.1 easier to use. These include large text, high-contrast themes, and an on-screen magnifier for people with vision problems to help with the keyboard, mouse, and even using the PC with just voice control or without a screen. You access the *Ease of Access* settings by clicking the *Settings* charm and then clicking *Change PC Settings* in the bottom right corner of your screen. In this section I will detail each of the Ease of Access settings.

- **Narrator** (Figure 7-7) will read text and other items on screen to you when you move your finger or mouse over them or highlight text. When pages load, such as in apps or on a web page, text will be read automatically.

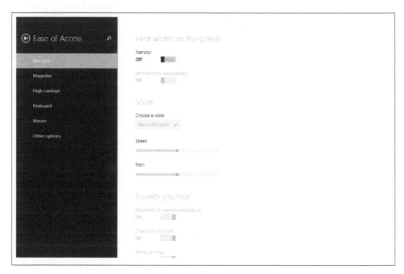

Figure 7-7. The Narrator will read items on screen to you

Some quick and useful commands for using the Narrator with your keyboard and with touch can be seen in Table 7-1.

Table 7-1. Narrator Commands in Windows 8.1

Action	With the Keyboard	With Touch
"Click" or select an object	Space bar or Enter key	Double tap
Double click and object on the desktop	Space bar or Enter key	Triple tap
Move to next / previous item	Caps Lock + left or right cursor	Flick left / right with finger
Read current desktop window	Caps Lock + W	Swipe up with three fingers
Read the currently selected item	Caps Lock + D	
Read the whole document	Caps Lock + H	

Action	With the Keyboard	With Touch
Repeat that	Caps Lock + V	
Move around the screen / scroll	Tab + Cursor keys in any direction	Swipe with two fingers in any direction
Stop narrator from reading	Ctrl	Tap once with two fingers
Display narrator controls		Tap with four fingers

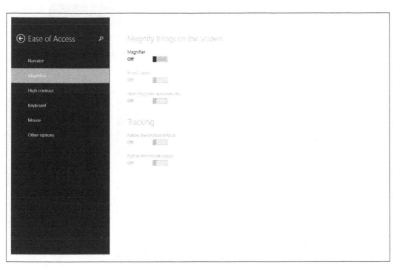

Figure 7-8. The Magnifier makes things in screen easier to read

- **Magnifier** (Figure 7-8) is used to make items on screen larger and easier to read. The magnifier zooms in on the screen, effectively making the desktop or apps larger than your PC's monitor. A magnifying glass control will appear on your screen (Figure 7-9), which, if you click or tap it, will reveal the full magnifier controls (Figure 7-10). On this control panel are zoom controls and a views menu that you can use to dock the zoom lens to the bottom of your screen. You can turn off the Magnifier by closing this control window.

Figure 7-9. The Magnifier appears on screen as a magnifying glass

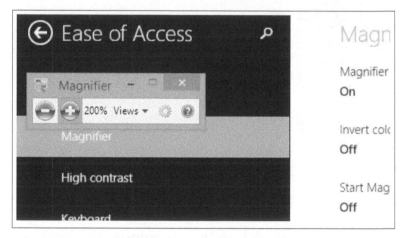

Figure 7-10. Click the magnifying glass for full Magnifier controls

- **High Contrast** (Figure 7-11) allows you to set color schemes for the desktop and apps where the contrast between background and foreground items is very pronounced. This can make things much easier to see and text easier to read.

Figure 7-11. You can turn on High Contrast color schemes

- **Keyboard** includes four main options.

  - Displaying the on-screen keyboard all of the time

  - Turning on *Sticky keys* which allow you to activate keyboard shortcuts such as *Ctrl + C* by pressing one key at a time instead of both together

  - *Toggle keys* which plays a sound when you press the Caps Lock, Num(ber) Lock, or Scroll Lock keys

  - *Filter keys* ignores multiple keystrokes, useful if you find yourself hitting a key twice or more instead of just once

- **Mouse** Figure 7-12 includes high-contrast options to make the mouse pointer more visible, an option to use your keyboard's cursor keys to move the mouse pointer, and the ability to slow down the mouse when you also hold down the *Ctrl* key

Figure 7-12. There are high-contrast mouse pointers available

- **Other options** include whether Windows 8.1 animates windows and apps when they are opened or closed and how long pop-up notification stay on the screen

Personalizing the Lock Screen

You can personalize the lock screen by clicking or tapping the *Lock screen* tile on the front page of PC Settings. Here you can change the picture on the Lock screen Figure 7-13 and also use the Lock screen as a digital photo frame, which I showed you how to do in Chapter 6.

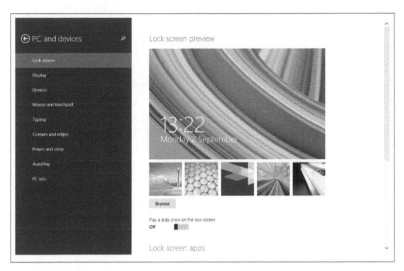

Figure 7-13. You can customize the Lock screen

In the *Lock screen apps* section you can choose which apps are allowed to display live information on the lock screen. This can include how many new emails and social network messages you have waiting for you. You can also choose one app to display more detailed information, such as forthcoming appointments. If you want, you can also remove one or all apps from the Lock screen, preventing them from displaying information there.

At the bottom of the Lock screen options is a switch to turn on and off the ability to swipe downward with your mouse or finger at the lock screen to activate your PC's camera (if it has one). This allows you to use the camera on a device such as a tablet without having to unlock the PC first.

Start Your PC Direct to the Desktop

If you are more of a desktop user than an app user you can set Windows 8.1 to automatically go to the desktop every time your PC starts. To do this, *right-click* in a blank space on the desktop Taskbar and select *Properties* from the options that appear. An options window will pop-up (Figure 7-14) in which you should click the *Navigation* tab.

Figure 7-14. You can tell Windows 8.1 to start directly to the desktop

To start Windows 8.1 to the desktop, check *Go to the desktop instead or Start when I sign in*. You can also configure the All Apps view in interesting ways here as well. The option *Show the Apps view automatically when I go to Start* will disable the Start screen completely. If you check this option, pressing the Windows key on your keyboard, on the Taskbar, or in the Charms will take you straight to the All Apps view instead.

If you check the *List desktop apps first in the Apps view when it's sorted by category* option, then your desktop programs will be listed in the All Apps view *ahead* of your Windows 8.1 apps. This settings requires, as the option says, that you sort the All Apps view by category, and you can find out how to do this in Chapter 4

Summary

As you can see, Windows 8.1 can be configured in a number of ways, including starting the PC directly to the desktop if desired. In Chapter 8 I'll begin showing you how to be productive with Windows by

---

setting up and using printers, network devices, projectors, and second displays.

Connecting To and Using Extra Hardware with Your Computer

In Chapter 6, I showed you how to import your digital photographs to your Windows 8.1 computer and how you can view them and perform some basic editing on them using the Photos app and Windows Photo Gallery. At some point, however, you might want to print some photographs or documents or connect your computer to external hardware. Let's start with printers.

Top Tips from This Chapter

1. Windows 8.1 can automatically detect and install wireless printers.

2. You can access network storage drives easily in File Explorer.

3. Windows 8.1 supports new multiscreen features, including panoramic wallpapers.

Attaching and Using a Printer

Windows 8.1 can automatically detect and install printers, even ones that are on your home or work WiFi network. You might find that the first time you want to print something that the printer has already been automatically installed.

You can check if your printer (or other external hardware) is installed by opening *PC Settings* and clicking/touching the *PC & Devices* section and then clicking *Devices* (Figure 8-1). You will see a list of all installed hardware on the right side of the screen, and at the top of the list is an *Add a device* button that you can click/touch to add something that hasn't been installed already.

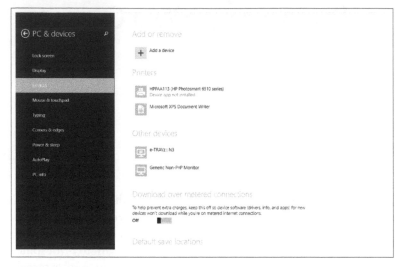

Figure 8-1. The Devices Panel in PC Settings

 To connect a wireless printer or other wireless network device to your home network, press the *WPS* button on both the printer and on your home Internet router to pair the devices. Check the documentation that came with your printer and router to see if this feature is supported on your devices and where the button is located.

When you click/touch the *Add a device* button, Windows 8.1 will search for devices connected directly to your computer via a cable and also for devices that are connected to your network. When Windows finds the device, it will appear in a list of new hardware, and Windows 8.1 will try to install it automatically.

To help with installing printers, make sure your computer is connected to the Internet when you connect the printer, so that Windows 8.1 can download the necessary software to install the printer correctly.

Sometimes a printer does not automatically install, or perhaps doesn't install correctly. If this happens, then Windows 8.1 includes a utility to help you manage and reinstall the devices. This is called the *Devices and Printers* panel (Figure 8-2), and you can open it by searching for *device* using the Search charm.

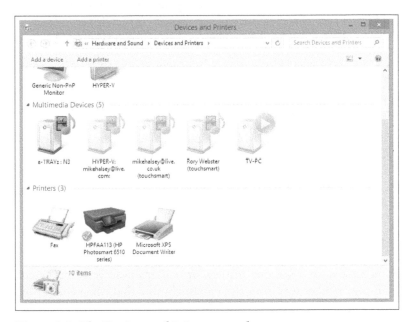

Figure 8-2. The Devices and Printers panel

Sometimes, and this is possible with WiFi network printers that Windows 8.1 has installed incorrectly, you might need to remove a printer or other device before you can reinstall it. Look for it in the list of installed devices, and if it appears in the list, right-click (or tap and hold) it, and from the options that appear, select *Remove Device*.

You can now click/touch the *Add a Printer* link near the top left of the Devices and Printers panel and Windows 8.1 will automatically search for printers that are both attached to the computer or that are on your network.

 Printers and other devices usually come with a CD or DVD containing software and drivers. If you put this disk in your computer's DVD or Blu-Ray drive, Windows 8.1 will ask you what you want to do. Select the *Run Setup* option to install your hardware.

The biggest difference between Windows 8.1 automatically installing printers and other devices and doing it yourself through the Devices and Printers panel is that you can specify the correct driver to install, making sure that the hardware works correctly with your computer.

After you have selected the device to install, Windows 8.1 will ask if you want to install the device automatically or *Browse my computer for driver software*. It is this second option that you want to select. Make sure the driver CD that came with your hardware is in your DVD drive.

A *Browse* button will appear. Click/Touch this and navigate to the CD or DVD, where the drivers for your hardware can be found. Make sure you have checked the *Include subfolders* box in this panel so that Windows 8.1 searches the entire disk. When you are ready, click/touch the *Next* button to install your device.

Setting the Default Printer

If you have more than one printer, or perhaps if an error occurred when your printer was installed, you might find that when you try to print something, it's either not printing, printing on the wrong printer, or opening a "save" window on your screen instead. This happens because the *default* printer has not been set correctly. You can identify the default printer, as it will have a green check mark on its icon in the Devices and Printers panel.

To rectify this, open the *Devices and Printers* panel and then *right-click* (or tap and hold) on the printer you want to print from as the default printer. When options appear, click/touch *Set as default printer*. Every print job will now be sent to this printer on your computer.

Printing in Windows 8.1

The way you print in Windows depends on whether you're printing from an app or from a desktop program. The latter will normally have a *Print* option under a menu, normally the *File* menu, on a ribbon tab (such as with Microsoft Office) or as a separate button. The style, size, and location of such buttons and options can vary widely.

Printing in Windows 8.1 apps is much simpler. You print by opening the *Devices* charm and then clicking *Print*. You will be shown a list of printers (and compatible other devices such as PDF file writers and fax machines) that you can print to. Click the printer you want to use, and the main printing options will appear (Figure 8-3).

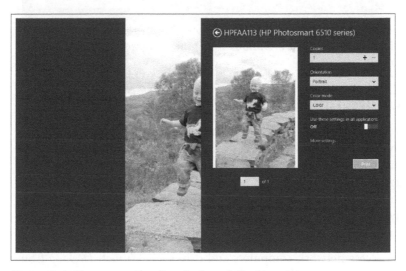

Figure 8-3. You can print directly from Windows 8.1 apps

The options you see will vary depending on the features on your particular printer, though the main controls of how many copies you want and the paper orientation will likely always be visible. Below these main options is a *More options* link that you can click to get access to additional options, such as duplex (double-sided) printing, paper type, and size and print quality (Figure 8-4).

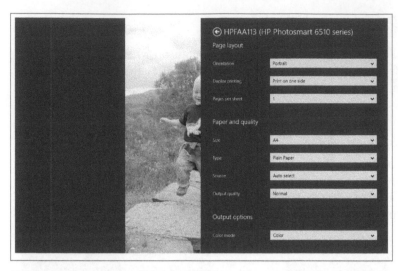

Figure 8-4. The More Options link provides great control over your printing

Connecting to Network Storage and Devices

You might have network storage in your home that you want to be able to use with your Windows 8.1 computer. This can include USB hard disks that you plug into some Internet routers to provide shared storage and backup for people in your home. This can be especially useful for sharing files between different computers or for having a location away from your main computer to back up documents, music, pictures, and videos.

To access network computers and drives, click/touch *Desktop* from the Start screen and on the Taskbar that runs along the bottom of the desktop, click/touch the yellow folder icon to open File Explorer.

In the left-hand panel, as seen in Figure 8-5, you have quick links to your Favorite links, HomeGroup, and This PC. At the bottom of this list is a *Network* link. Click/Touch this and File Explorer will show you all the available network computers and drives (remember, they need to be switched on to be visible).

Figure 8-5. Accessing Network Storage in File Explorer

You can save network drives to your Start screen to give you easy access in the future. *Right-click* on a network drive and from the options that appear, click/touch *Pin to Start*. A shortcut link to the network storage will then be placed on your Start screen.

Using a Second Screen with Your Computer

Sometimes, and especially if you use your Windows 8.1 computer in a home office, you will want to attach a second screen to the computer. You can attach this to your computer via a VGA or DVI video cable (both of which are a D-shaped plug in either blue or white) or via an HDMI video lead. You should check the documentation that came with your computer to see which video ports are supported.

Windows 8.1 will automatically detect the second screen and perhaps even give you a picture on it straight away. You can also choose what is displayed on the second screen manually, however, by opening the Charms menu and clicking/touching *Devices* and then click *Project*. Now you should click/touch the *Second screen* option.

You now have four options for how to extend your screen to the second display (Figure 8-6).

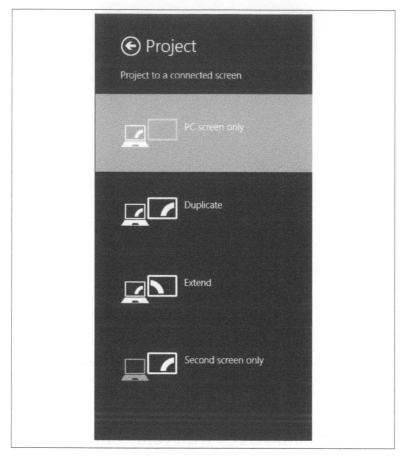

Figure 8-6. Using a second screen with your Computer

- *PC Screen only* turns off the second screen.
- *Duplicate* will display the same thing on both screens.
- *Extend* will use both monitors together as a big, extended display.
- *Second Screen only* turns off the display on your main computer.

Whichever you choose, when you unplug the second screen, your computer's display will return to normal.

Customizing Your Multiscreen Display

Windows 8.1 includes some new features for multidisplay computers, including support for panoramic wallpapers on the desktop. To take advantage of this, *right-click* anywhere in empty space on the desktop and then click/touch *Personalize* from the options that appear.

At the bottom of the window that appears next, click/touch *Desktop background*. You will see some multiscreen wallpapers, and you can click/touch the *Browse* button to use one or several of your own. When you have selected the correct image, click/touch the *Picture position* button at the bottom left of the panel and then click/touch *Span* from the available options (Figure 8-7).

Figure 8-7. Setting a multiscreen wallpaper

Summary

Windows 8.1 is excellent at automatically detecting new hardware and installing it for you, even network printers that earlier versions of Windows haven't been able to do. It doesn't always get it right, but the controls available for you to fix problems are simply laid out and easy to use.

Moving on from connecting a second display to your computer, in Chapter 9, I'll show you how to set up and use your Windows 8.1 computer for work, so that you can be at your most productive.

Using Windows 8.1 for Work

Whether it's for work, college, or personal finance, Windows has always been the choice for being productive and getting things done. In Chapter 4, I showed you how you can snap two desktop windows side by side, which is a great way to compare two documents, and it's a feature that I use all the time.

There is much more that you can do with the desktop, though, and I'll show you how in this chapter. There are several ways to get Microsoft Office. If you are using a Windows 8.1 PC, laptop, ultrabook or tablet and you have not purchased a copy of Microsoft Office, you can use the free Office web apps, which are quite fully featured. If you are using a Windows RT PC, you will find full copies of Word, Excel, OneNote, PowerPoint, and Outlook pre-installed.

Top Tips from This Chapter

1. Windows RT comes with full versions of Word, Excel, OneNote, PowerPoint, and Outlook.

2. The Ribbon can be operated by touch, and its tabs group similar functions together.

3. The Mobility Center has tools that can dramatically extend the battery life of a laptop or tablet.

Using Microsoft Office in Windows 8.1

As I've said in the introduction to this chapter, there are different ways to use Microsoft Office depending on what version of Windows 8.1 you have. Microsoft Office is based around the company's *Ribbon* interface, which was first seen in Office 2007. This is an alternative to the older-style drop-down menus as a way to access a program's features. If you're not used to it, then test out some of the desktop programs supplied with Windows 8.1, including File Explorer, Paint, and WordPad. These all include the Ribbon. I will show you how to use the Ribbon shortly.

Microsoft Office Web Apps

Windows 8.1 on desktops and laptops doesn't come with a version of Microsoft Office installed, but you might see links to the *Office Web Apps*. You can find them on the Internet at *http://office.microsoft.com/ web-apps*. These are based on Microsoft's new look for their latest version of Office and includes Word (Figure 9-1) and Excel. They look slightly different but are still based on the Ribbon interface.

Figure 9-1. Microsoft Word 2013

There are no limits to using the free version of the Office web apps, but you will need a live Internet connection to be able to use them.

You will probably find that the web apps do almost everything you need in terms of a basic word processor and spreadsheet.

Using Microsoft Office on Windows RT

If you've bought a Windows RT tablet, you might find a more comprehensive version of Office installed. The programs here are still feature-limited versions of the full Office suite, but they include Word, Excel, PowerPoint (for making presentations), OneNote (the note taking program that works very well on touch screens), and Outlook (for email).

 If you have bought a copy of Microsoft Office 2013, the programs you get are identical to those included with Windows RT (note that the Windows RT apps do exclude some business functionality).

These versions are fully featured, though in Windows RT they do exclude a small number of business-only features. This means that almost everything you can do in Microsoft Office 2013 on your main home or work PC you can also do in Microsoft Office RT.

The Ribbon Explained

The *Ribbon* is made up of tabs: *File, Home, Insert,* and so on, each of which, when clicked or touched, shows commands that are organized into groups (Figure 9-2). As you make the window bigger, more commands appear on the Ribbon, so to see all of the Ribbon commands, maximize the window to make it full screen. The maximize button is a small square in the top right of the window, next to the close button.

Figure 9-2. The Ribbon interface

Each version of an Office program has the same four tabs on the left side of the Ribbon:

- *File* is where you will find the new document and open and save commands.

- *Home* is where all of the text and other formatting commands can be found.

- *Insert* is where you have options to insert images and other items such as sound and video into documents.

- *Page Layout* is where you can control the size and other aspects of your document.

In the Microsoft Word web app, you will also see a *Mailings* tab where you can control mail merges, which can be very useful for small businesses, organizations, and groups to send letters and emails to many people. Microsoft Office 2013 and Office RT include additional tabs with more features and controls.

In the Microsoft Excel web app, you will see a *Formulas* tab, where you can add automatic calculations to your spreadsheets. Microsoft Office 2013 and Office RT include additional tabs with more features and controls.

Being Productive with Office

You create, open, and save files in all Microsoft Office apps by clicking the *File* tab. This takes you to a view with the main file control commands listed down the left of the window, with additional context-sensitive options, in the main panel of the window, as seen in Figure 9-1.

Some features in Microsoft Office can help you be very productive. In the very top left of the window, you will see the *Quick Access Toolbar*. Here are icons you can click/touch for some of the most common tasks (Figure 9-3). By default, there are icons for *Save*, *Undo*, and *Refresh*.

Figure 9-3. Tabs on the Ribbon

If you click/touch the down arrow to the right of these icons, you can add and remove icons from the menu by simply selecting them from the drop-down options menu that appears.

In the top right of the window, just below the minimize, maximize, and close buttons, you will see a small arrow (Figure 9-4). Clicking the arrow will minimize (or maximize) the buttons on the Ribbon so that it only appears when you click/touch on a Ribbon tab. Otherwise, it appears all the time. This can be useful if you have a small screen. There is also a Question Mark icon in the top right of the window that, when clicked, will display help.

Figure 9-4. Hiding the Ribbon and Help

In the bottom right of the window are controls for moving about within pages and viewing your document in different ways, but most importantly, you'll find the zoom control (Figure 9-5). You can use this to make your document larger or smaller in the window, which is useful if you find small text difficult to read or if you need to see more of the document on your screen.

Figure 9-5. Making things bigger or smaller

Using the Desktop in Windows 8.1

In Chapter 4, I showed you how to snap two desktop windows side by side. There is so much more you can do on the desktop, however.

For instance, if you don't want to keep switching back and forth between the Start screen and desktop when launching programs, you can *pin* programs directly onto the desktop Taskbar (the bar that runs along the bottom of the screen) so that they are there all the time, enabling you to get quick access to them.

To do this, right-click on a program (or touch and hold with your finger) on the Start screen or All Apps view, and from the App Bar click/touch *Pin to Taskbar*. You can select multiple programs at the same time and pin them all with the same click, but you cannot pin Windows 8.1 apps to the Taskbar, only desktop programs.

Program icons on the Taskbar also have their own *Jumplists*. You can access these by touching the icon and pushing upward or *right-clicking* with your mouse. Each Jumplist contains controls for things you can do with that program, such as launching another instance of it or closing it.

Jumplists also contain a list of recently opened files. You can *pin* a file to the Jumplist so that it always appears there (Figure 9-6). This can be useful if you have files that you need to access regularly. You can unpin files the same way.

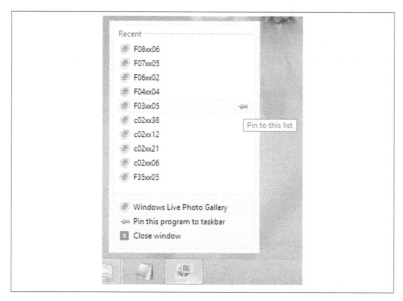

Figure 9-6. Pinning documents to Jumplists

You can also see thumbnail images of open programs, even if they are minimized from the Taskbar. This can be useful if you have many windows open on your desktop or are perhaps using a web browser with many tabs open at the same time. To do this, hover your mouse over an open program on the Taskbar and a thumbnail image of the program will appear (Figure 9-7).

Please note that you can't see thumbnail images of running desktop programs with a touch gesture.

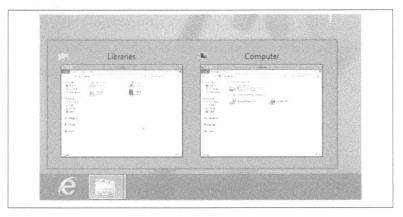

Figure 9-7. Viewing thumbnails of running programs

If you have a lot of windows open, moving your mouse over a thumbnail will temporarily hide all other windows and show you the one you have selected (even if it is minimized itself). You can then, if you want to, switch directly to that window by clicking the thumbnail.

Hiding and Restoring All the Open Desktop Windows

If you have a lot of windows open on your screen and you want to minimize them all, perhaps when you go for a break, you can click/touch with your mouse in the far right of the desktop Taskbar, to the right of the time and date. This will minimize all windows. You can then restore them all by clicking this area again. Moving your mouse cursor to the very bottom right of your screen will temporarily minimize every window. They will be restored when you move your mouse away from this area.

Connecting and Using Projectors and Second Screens

Windows 8.1 is excellent at detecting additional hardware, such as projectors and secondary displays. You can access these by opening the Charms menu and clicking *Devices* and then clicking *Project*.

Here you will see a list of additional displays available to your computer. This includes projectors, second screens, and wireless displays. Clicking on a display will bring up several options for that display (Figure 9-8).

- *PC Screen Only* will turn off the image to the secondary display.
- *Duplicate* will put the same image on both displays.
- *Extend* will use the second screen to extend your desktop.
- *Second Screen Only* will use only the second display until you unplug it.

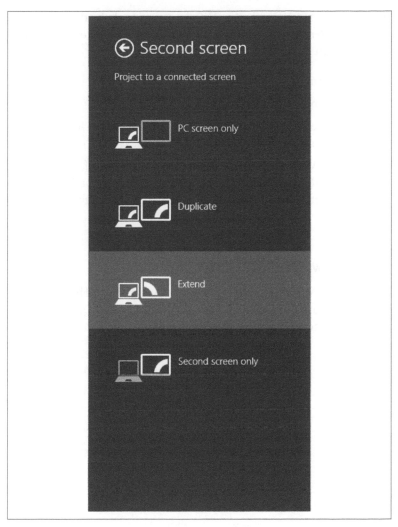

Figure 9-8. Choosing how to extend your display to a second screen

Maximizing Battery Life on Your Laptop or Tablet

Battery life is always an important issue for computers. If you have a Windows RT tablet, you may be getting 10 hours or more out of your battery, but on a laptop or Windows 8.1 Pro ultrabook, you'll more likely be getting just 4 or 5 hours.

You can maximize your battery life by using tools in the *Windows Mobility Center*, which I will talk about in the next section, but other things you can do include:

- Turn off any keyboard backlight.

- Turn down your screen brightness.

- Don't leave programs and apps that will read/write to your hard disk running, such as music players

- Turn off WiFi (if your computer has a WiFi on/off switch) and your mobile broadband when you're not using it. You can also do this by switching on Airplane mode. See Chapter 2 for how to do this.

The Windows Mobility Center

The Windows Mobility Center (Figure 9-9) can be found by searching for *Mobility* from the Search charm. It is the best place to go to balance your battery life with on-the-road performance.

Figure 9-9. The Windows Mobility Center

Here you can adjust your display brightness, speaker volume, and more. Some of the more interesting and useful features are:

- *Battery Status* enables you to choose several different battery modes for your computer, including a power-saving mode.

- *Presentation Settings*, if turned on while using your computer to give a presentation, will silence all desktop and other alerts. This includes pop-up messages informing you of new email. Windows will also be prevented from turning off the display during a period of inactivity or going to sleep with this mode activated.

Summary

Windows 8.1 contains excellent tools and utilities for being productive and working for long periods away from a power socket. The inclusion of full Microsoft Office programs in Windows RT is a welcome bonus for productivity, and the Windows Mobility Center is a great tool for managing your battery life.

These features, coupled with some of the excellent and sometimes hidden ways you can interact with and use programs on the desktop, make Windows 8.1 a great tool for being productive, whatever you need it for and wherever you are.

Sometimes you will want to use older software with Windows 8.1, perhaps software that you're really comfortable with or that you need for a specific task. In Chapter 10, I will show you how to make sure this software runs properly in Windows 8.1.

Using Older Software and Programs

Even though there are already a great many new apps specifically for Windows 8, many of which are completely free, you might still have older desktop programs that you like to use or even brand new desktop programs.

There's a *Desktop* tile on the Windows 8.1 Start screen, but how do you install desktop programs? Do you get it all from the Windows Store, and how can you make sure that the older programs you've come to either love or rely on still work?

 You can only install desktop programs on your tablet if it is running Windows 8.1 Pro. If you want to use desktop software, you should ask if it runs the Pro version before making your purchase.

Top Tips from This Chapter

1. Not all Windows XP programs will work in Windows 8.1, but you can turn on *Compatibility Mode* for programs that don't work properly.

2. Do not allow program installations unless you *specifically* intended to install it because it could be malware.

3. You can uninstall apps and programs directly from the Start screen by right-clicking them, or tapping and dragging down.

Why Won't My Program Run?

Some programs designed for Windows XP just won't work in Windows 8.1. When Microsoft released Windows Vista in 2006, they made fundamental changes to the way Windows works. This included introducing completely new features to the operating system and removing others.

Because of this, some programs designed for Windows 98 and Windows XP need to use operating system features that just don't exist any more, and that were removed to improve security or reliability.

Windows Tablets and Desktop Programs

If you have a Windows RT tablet, you will not be able to install desktop programs onto the computer. The desktop still exists, and you will know that you have this type of tablet because you will have feature-limited versions of Microsoft's Office programs Word, Excel, PowerPoint, OneNote, and Outlook already installed.

The reason you can't install desktop programs on Windows 8.1 tablets is because of incompatibilities with the different type of hardware your tablet has inside it. Simply put, Windows desktop programs won't run on this hardware because it is incompatible with it. You can still install desktop programs on a Windows 8.1 Pro tablet, though.

Installing Desktop Programs in Windows 8.1

So where do you get desktop programs and how do you install them? It is most common to download programs from the Internet, and some desktop programs can be downloaded from the Windows Store, but you can also install programs from a USB flash drive or a CD/DVD.

When you plug a disk, a USB flash drive, or another type of drive into your Windows 8.1 computer, a pop-up alert will appear in the top right of your screen asking what you want to do with it (Figure 10-1).

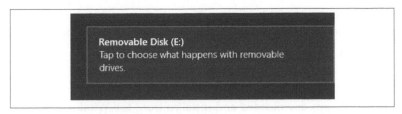

Figure 10-1. Windows alerts you when you insert a disk or drive

You are given several choices in this pop-up alert (Figure 10-2). If you intend to install programs, you will probably see the option to *Run Setup.exe*, which is the usual name for a program installer.

Figure 10-2. Do you want to run setup.exe?

You will also see options to *Open a folder...* to view the contents of the disk. You may want to do this if you are copying files from the disk, or if Windows 8.1 has not recognized the correct program to install.

If you tell Windows to install the programs, you are taken to the desktop and the program will install from there. You will be presented with a security panel asking you to confirm that you do *actually* want to install this program. This security feature is here to help prevent viruses and other malware from making changes to your computer.

Be Careful What Programs You Install

While all apps downloaded and installed from the Windows Store have been scanned for malware by Microsoft, programs you install or download from another source do not come with a guarantee that it won't contain a virus.

Try to avoid installing trial programs and/or too many programs. Installing trialware means that you are likely to end up with lots of expired programs that won't run (usually after 30 days), will take up space, and could cause other problems. Installing too many programs could cause your computer to become unstable over time.

Installing a Program in Compatibility Mode

Windows 8.1 is very good at detecting if programs might not run correctly—for instance, if the program you wish to install was designed and written for an earlier version of Windows, such as XP. If this happens, it will alert you that there might be problems with the program and that it might not run properly (Figure 10-3).

Figure 10-3. Installing programs in Compatibility Mode

If you know the program works fine in Windows 8.1 (most programs that work in Windows 7 will also work in Windows 8.1) then click/

---

touch *This program installed correctly*, but if you are not sure, click/ touch *Reinstall using recommended settings.* Windows 8.1 will then reinstall the program, applying different settings that make older programs more likely to run without problems.

Troubleshooting Program Compatibility

If you are still having problems getting programs to run properly, you can set the compatibility for the program manually. Windows 8.1 provides a wizard to help you through this issue (Figure 10-4). To set the compatibility for a program manually, follow these instructions:

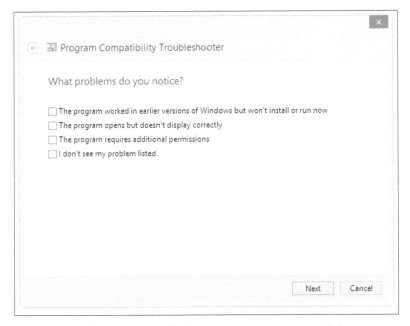

Figure 10-4. Manually troubleshooting program compatibility

1. From the Start screen or All Apps view, *right-click* the relevant program.
2. From the App Bar, click/touch *Open File Location* and a window will open with the program highlighted.
3. *Right-click* (touch and hold) the program and an options menu will appear.
4. Select *Troubleshoot Compatibility* and the Automatic Troubleshooter will appear.

5. Click/Touch the *Troubleshoot Program* button.

You are now asked a series of questions about how the program worked in the past. At the end of this process, Windows automatically sets the compatibility for the program and asks you to test it. If it still does not work, it will allow you to change the compatibility settings and try again.

Running Programs on the Windows Desktop

Icons for installed desktop programs appear on your Start screen. In Chapter 4, I showed you how you can arrange and organize Tiles and icons on the Start screen, including hiding them. Some desktop programs will also install utilities (including uninstallers), which you may want to hide to keep the Start screen tidy and easy to use.

You can run a desktop program from the Start screen by clicking/ touching it. If it is a desktop program you are starting, you will immediately be taken to the desktop, and the program will be started.

Making the Best of the Taskbar

In Chapter 4, I showed you how you can pin desktop programs to the Windows 8.1 desktop Taskbar. If you spend a lot of time working on the desktop, this is a good way to avoid having to switch between the Start screen and the desktop to run a program.

When a program is running, you can also *right-click* its desktop icon and select *Pin to Taskbar* (or *Unpin from Taskbar*).

Uninstalling Desktop Programs in Windows 8.1

Uninstalling programs in Windows 8.1 is, if anything, slightly easier than in previous versions of Windows. To uninstall a program, *right-click* (or *tap and drag downward*) its icon on the Start screen or in the All Apps view, and from the App Bar, select *Uninstall*.

Apps will be uninstalled automatically, but if you are uninstalling a program, you will be taken to the *Programs and Features* window on the desktop. Here, you will need to find the program by looking for its name in the list.

Once you have found the program, click/tap on the program name. In the toolbar above the list of programs, you will see an *Uninstall* or a *Remove* option appear. Click/Touch this to uninstall the program (Figure 10-5).

Figure 10-5. Uninstalling a desktop program

 You can click/touch on the column headers *Name*, *Installed On*, etc., to sort the installed programs in different ways; for example, showing the most recently installed programs at the top of the list.

Summary

Windows 8.1 is compatible with most of the programs that ran on Windows 7 and Windows Vista. Sadly, it is not compatible with all Windows XP programs. You might find that just small parts of an older program fail to work. I have an old program I like to use that does this and I can get by with it in Windows 8.1 because the bit that doesn't work is a feature I don't really need.

The compatibility settings can help make older programs run in Windows 8.1 but if, in the case of the program I like to use, it calls a Windows feature that has long since been removed, there's nothing that can be done to make it work properly.

I've written throughout this book and in this chapter about the dangers of having malware on your computer. In Chapter 11, I'll show you how to keep your family safe when using your computer and going online.

Keeping You and Your Family Safe

One of the biggest challenges people face when using computers is keeping safe when they're on the Internet. How do you keep malware off your computer, how can you tell a fake website from a real one, and how do you keep your children safe from inappropriate web content and unsuitable games?

These are concerns, not just for parents but also for every Internet user. In this chapter, I want to show you how Windows 8.1 can help keep you, your friends, and your family safe.

Top Tips from This Chapter

1. Each user should have their own account to separate her personal files and Internet favorites.

2. Criminals will try and trick you into installing malware/viruses; do not click/touch things casually.

3. The Family Safety features in Windows 8.1 can help keep your children safe online.

Setting Up Additional Users on Your Computer

When you first use Windows 8.1, you will be asked to create a user account, either a local one on the computer or one created using a Microsoft account; this will have the same login you use for a Hotmail or Live email account or for your Xbox.

When you set up a new user on your PC you are asked if this is a child's account. Check this box to automatically turn on the *Activity Report*. This is an easy-to-read summary of what your child has been looking at on the Internet, and it can be accessed in the main *Family Safety* window. See below for details of how to open this.

When you are using Windows 8.1 in a family environment, it's always a good idea to give each user his own user account, but what is the difference between a local account and a Microsoft Account?

- A local account is stored only on a single computer, and it's exclusive to that computer. It only gives a person access to that one computer. It doesn't come with an email address, nor does it come with the ability to use the Windows Store or purchase apps or games.

- A Microsoft account synchronizes your computer with your email, calendar, and contacts, and also allows you to buy apps and games from the Store. This account type also allows you to log into multiple Windows 8.1 computers and automatically see all of *your* own Internet favorites, email, and apps on each and every computer.

This doesn't mean that anybody with a Hotmail or Xbox Live account can simply gain access to your computer. You need to specifically give them their own account first, and I will show you how to do this shortly.

The other benefit to people having their own user accounts is that it keeps each person's files and Internet favorites separate, so they don't get mixed up and one person's files can't be deleted by another person accidentally.

To create a new user account, you need to go to *PC Settings*. Remember, you get to this by opening the Charms, clicking/touching Settings, then clicking/touching Change PC Settings.

1. Click/Touch *Accounts* in the left-hand panel
2. Click/Touch +Other Accounts_ (Figure 11-1).
3. Click/Touch *Add a user* in the main panel.
4. To add someone who already has a Microsoft Account, enter her email address. You will need to be connected to the Internet at this point. However, the user won't need to be present, and you won't need to know their password. You can set up their account, and

they will be asked for their password the first time they log in to the PC.

5. To sign up for a Microsoft Account, click/touch *Sign up for a new email address.* You will need to be connected to the Internet to create an account.

6. To create a local user account, click/touch *Don't want this user to sign in with a Microsoft Account?* This does not require Internet access.

When you create a local account, you will be asked for a password. This is required with a Microsoft Account, but it is optional for a local account. For example, you might not want to set a password for young children because it is easy for them to forget, and do they need their own password on your computer anyway?

 When starting your computer, if you do not see the user account you want displayed, click/touch the back button next to the user picture to display all the user accounts on the computer you can log in with.

Figure 11-1. The Users panel in PC Settings.bmp

Viruses, Malware, and Phishing Explained

So you've created your user accounts and you're browsing the Internet. Are you safe doing this? Well, there are criminals who want to trick you into installing viruses onto your computer and surrendering personal and sensitive information.

I'm going to lump all nasties and meanies together under the *malware* name, but technically, malware is a malicious program, file, and email intended to steal your personal information (credit card details, passwords, date of birth, mother's maiden name) or to trick you into revealing them yourself.

Malware spreads in several ways:

- Websites that try to trick you into downloading a file, pretending that you need it to play video or perform a specific action.
- Downloaded files from file-sharing websites; these are commonly laden with malware.
- Infected email attachments, Adobe PDF files, or Word, Excel, or PowerPoint documents are common targets.
- Infected storage devices, such as USB flash drives.

The simple rule is that if you did not visit a website to download something, DON'T download anything. If you go to YouTube and receive a message saying a *codec* is required to watch a video, it's lying. If you go to any other website that tries to download files to your computer, just say *No*.

If you are ever in doubt about attachments sent by a friend or colleague, just email them asking if they intended to send it, before you open it.

Phishing is the act of sending emails that try to trick you into believing that they're from a reputable bank or website (such as PayPal). They say they need you to log in to confirm your security or personal details. The link they provide will always take you to a fake website, and your details will be stolen.

The rule here is that NO reputable bank or website will EVER email you asking you to log in to confirm your security details.

Fake Antivirus Software: Be Alert

One other thing to be aware of is when a website says they have scanned your computer and found malware, but their software can get rid of it for you. NO website is capable of scanning your computer for malware without your express permission. These websites are *always* fake, and their software is malware intended to scam you out of your credit card and other personal details.

Using Windows Defender to Keep Your Computer Safe

The good news is that all versions of Windows 8.1 come with anti-malware software built in. It's call Windows Defender, and you can find it by searching for *defender* at the Start screen. You probably won't need to open it, though, because it will update itself and scan regularly in the background.

Windows Defender is updated through Windows Update, so it is important not to turn that off! I will show you how to use Windows Update in Chapter 12.

If you do want to open Windows Defender, it has a friendly interface that changes color from green to amber and red to alert you to its current status (Figure 11-2). If it is not currently up to date, an *Update* button will appear on the front screen, and you can choose to run either a *Quick Scan*, which scans Windows and your documents, or a *Full Scan*, which scans every file on your computer for malware.

Figure 11-2. Windows Defender

Browsing Safely with Internet Explorer 11

Internet Explorer is very good at alerting you to both safe and unsafe websites when you visit them, and also to malware and malicious downloads. The first thing it does is highlight the actual name of the website. In Figure 11-3, you can see that the name *paypal.com* is bolder than the rest of the text. This is so you can tell if you are at the correct website, perhaps because you've clicked on a link in an email.

Figure 11-3. Internet Explorer tells you when websites are safe or not

Whenever you visit a website for banking or shopping, you will also see a padlock symbol on the right of the address bar on any page that requires you to type personal details. This sometimes also appears with the name of the company, and this is assurance that a valid security certificate is owned by this company and that all your personal details are encrypted before your web browser sends them on.

You will also see in Figure 11-3 that the address bar has turned green. This is Internet Explorer's way of telling you that this website is known to be safe. If the address bar turns red, then you are visiting a website that is known to be insecure and may contain malware. You should leave the website immediately.

Internet Explorer also scans all the documents and files you download. It does this using Windows Defender and a feature in Internet Explorer called *SmartScreen*. This checks all downloads against lists of known safe and unsafe files. If it thinks a file might be potentially dangerous to you or your computer, it will alert you and ask if you want to continue.

Setting Up and Using Family Safety

When you set up a user account, Windows 8.1 will ask you if this account is for a child. If it is, Windows can give you reports showing what that user has done online, but this doesn't stop them from visiting inappropriate websites or viewing unsuitable content to begin with. That is where the Windows 8.1 Family Safety features come in.

If you have young children, you will want to keep them safe online. Windows 8.1 contains an excellent and fully featured set of Family Safety options in which you can choose:

- What times of day and on what days they can use the computer
- What types of games they can play
- What websites they can visit

You can open the Family Safety area by searching for *family* at the Start screen. You will find it under the *Settings* search results.

 To use Family Safety, your child must already have his own user account created in PC Settings and your own user account *must* have a password on it. This prevents the child from changing the parental control settings himself.

Always use strong passwords. It is preferable to use a password that is ten characters or more in length and contains a mixture of upper- and lowercase letters, as well as numbers and symbols. (Remember, you can substitute some numbers and symbols for letters, e.g., 1 = i or l, & = a, 5 = s or S.) I will show you more ways to create a strong password in Chapter 13.

At the main Family Safety panel, click/touch on the child's account for which you want to create controls. You need to set up each child's account individually. On the right of the Family Safety window is a link to *View [the] Activity Report.* This is an easy to read summary of what your child has been looking at online and is available if you marked the account as a child's account when it was created.

You will see a button to turn the Family Safety on or off for this child (see Figure 11-4). You can also turn activity reporting for the child on and off. These activity reports are available at any time by clicking the *View activity reports* link on the right side of the page.

Figure 11-4. Setting Family Safety

There are four main categories of Family Safety controls you can set. The allowed programs category is quite complex and you will probably not want to use it, but the other categories are excellent and include the following.

Windows Web Filter

Here, you can block certain types of websites on the account, based on five easy-to-understand *filtering levels* (Figure 11-5):

- *Allow list only*, where you manually specify the website that can be visited, although this can be time consuming
- *Designed for children*, in which all adult websites and content are blocked
- *General interest* expands the list of child-friendly websites for slightly older children of school age
- *Online communication* allows children to access email and social networking websites
- *Warn an adult* will provide unlimited access but will warn the child when she might be visiting an adult website

There is also a check box that allows you to block children from downloading files from the Internet. This can help prevent them from inadvertently downloading malware to your PC.

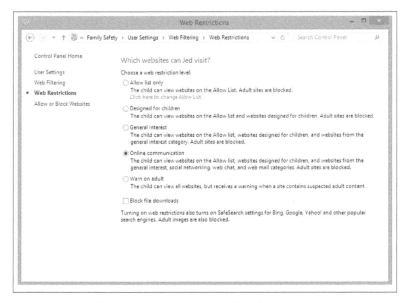

Figure 11-5. Allowing or blocking specific websites

You can also click/touch the link *Allow or Block Websites* in the left-hand panel to customize the list of websites that children can and cannot visit. This is useful if a website is automatically blocked when you want to allow it or when a child might need it for school.

Time Limits

This is where you can control the time of day and days of the week that the child can use the computer, or just the maximum number of hours that the computer can be used each day (Figure 11-6). You can specify when the child can use the computer in the *Set curfew* controls by coloring in a chart. You can drag your finger or mouse around this chart to specify the blocks of time when the computer cannot be used.

Figure 11-6. You can specify when children can use a computer

The computer is not automatically shut down out of these times; the child is given plenty of warning by Windows 8.1 that he or she is coming to the end of the allocated time and that, perhaps, it is time for bed.

Games

Here, you can block certain games according to their rating so that only games that are rated as suitable for your child's age can be played. Note, however, that not all games are rated this way, and so some games might slip past this certification (Figure 11-7). This does not block Internet games that are played online and not directly installed on your computer.

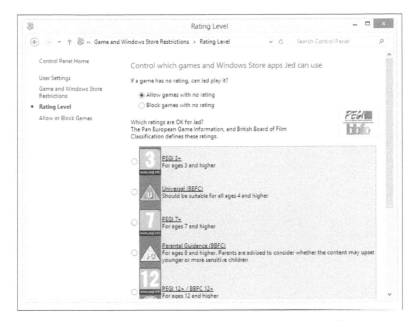

Figure 11-7. You can block unsuitable games in Family Safety

Summary

It's fairly straightforward to stay safe with Windows 8.1, because it not only comes with all the basic security a family needs, but out of the box, it's also set up the way you need it.

The Family Safety options in Windows 8.1 is an excellent way to keep your children safe online, and the lists of safe and unsafe websites that Windows 8 uses to determine which websites are suitable for your children to visit are being constantly monitored by Microsoft and security organizations. The ability to add or block specific websites from this list manually is an additional added bonus.

As is always the advice, it's best to take an interest in what your children do online so that you can monitor them and make sure that they're safe and not exposed to unsuitable material.

Now that you and your family are safe, in Chapter 12, I'll show you how you can keep your copy of Windows 8.1 running safely and smoothly so that it doesn't cause you problems.

Keeping Your Computer Running Smoothly

One of the biggest concerns facing home computer users is the thought that sooner or later something's going to go wrong, and either the computer won't start, or it will misbehave. This can result in being without your computer for a while and paying expensive repair costs.

As the author of *Troubleshoot and Optimize Windows 8 Inside Out*, I'd like to share with you some of the *best* ways that you can keep Windows 8.1 running smoothly and can rescue it easily in the event that something goes wrong.

Top Tips from This Chapter

1. Always keep a regular and up-to-date backup copy of your files!
2. You can *Refresh* Windows 8.1 easily to a working copy if it starts to malfunction.
3. You can create a *Recovery Drive* that can be used to rescue Windows 8.1 in the event that it won't start.

How to Keep Your Files Backed Up

Files and documents on your computer may be important, so if something disastrous happens to your computer or if you have to reinstall Windows from scratch, you'll be pretty upset if they are wiped. This is why the *most* important thing you can ever do with a computer is to keep regular backups of your files.

File History will back up everything in your user folders (Documents, Pictures, Music, and Video). It will not back up anything outside of these but you can add other folders to your Libraries to include them in the backup. I will show you how to use Libraries in Chapter 13.

Windows 8.1 includes an excellent backup program that you can find by opening PC Settings and then clicking *Update and Recovery*, followed by *File History*. File History can be set to automatically keep an updated copy of your files backed up, and is very easy to use (Figure 11-1). Additionally, File History keeps backup copies of files that have been changed and deleted. This can help you recover files you've made changes to but didn't mean to make or that are deleted accidentally.

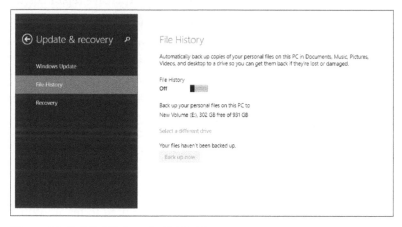

Figure 12-1. File History in PC Settings

The best place to keep a backup copy of your files is on an external hard disk. These are very cheap and can often be plugged in to your Internet router, which allows the files to be accessed by any computer in your home.

File History will look for a second hard disk or an external, e.g., USB, hard disk that it can use as your file backup. It can't store backups on the same hard disk on which Windows 8.1 is installed, and this is to help guarantee your file resilience.

The first time File History runs, it will create a full backup of all of your files. After this, it will run on a schedule, normally every hour but this can be altered in the full File History controls from the Control Panel, and it will back up every file that has changed or been deleted.

 If you want to use a network location, such as an external hard disk plugged into your Internet router, you will need to run File History from the desktop Control Panel. Here you have much more control, such as being able to store your backups in a specific folder on a hard disk or network location. When you are viewing the full File History controls, Figure 12-2, if no USB or other attached or internal hard disk is found, you will be prompted for a network location, perhaps a shared USB hard disk that's plugged into your Internet router. Finer controls are available through the *Select drive* link on the left of the window.

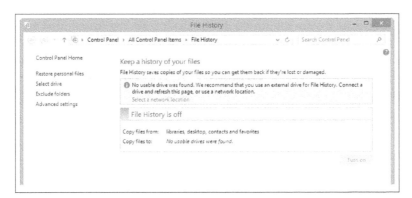

Figure 12-2. The full File History controls

File History is very good at regulating the hard disk space it uses, automatically deleting older version of files if it's running out of free space. If you want to delete some older, now unwanted, versions of files or if you want finer control over the backup process, you can click *Advanced settings* from the File History window in the Control Panel. Additionally, clicking the *Exclude folders* link lets you stop specified files from being included in the File History backup.

If you need to restore a file at any time, you can either click *Restore personal files* in the File History window in the Control Panel or, in File Explorer you can click the *History* button under the *Home* tab on the ribbon (Figure 12-3).

Figure 12-3. Accessing File History from File Explorer

When you are in the File History restore window ((Figure 12-4) you can navigate just as you would in File Explorer using the address bar at the top of the screen to move to the folder containing the file or files you wish to restore. At the bottom of the screen are back and forward buttons that will take you back and forward in time for when the backups were made (and you will see the backup date and time change at the top of the window).

Figure 12-4. Restoring files using File History

You can select multiple files in sequence by clicking the first one and then holding down the *Shift* key and clicking the last, or you can select multiple files by holding down the *Ctrl* key when you click each one to select it. To restore the files, click/tap the large green restore button in the bottom center of the window.

Refreshing Windows 8.1

While it's easy to backup and restore your files, it also simple to repair your copy of Windows 8.1 if things get a bit wobbly or unstable. This uses a feature called *Refresh*, which restores your copy of Windows 8.1 to the working state it was in when you first started using it without affecting or deleting any of your files, user accounts, or main Windows settings.

You'll have noticed I said your *main* Windows settings, as not everything is included. You will have to reinstall your apps, and I will show you a quick way to do this in Chapter 13, and you will also need to reinstall any desktop software you were using. So long as you sign into your PC with a Microsoft Account though, most other settings for the Start screen and desktop will be automatically reapplied from the backup Windows 8.1 automatically makes of these in the cloud.

To Refresh your PC, open PC Settings and then click/tap *Update & Recovery* ,then click/tap *Recovery*, and at the top of your screen you will see the text *Refresh your PC without affecting your files* (Figure 12-5). You can click the *Get Started* button to begin the Refresh process.

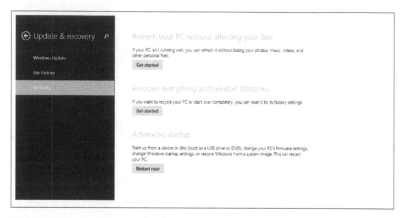

Figure 12-5. Starting Refresh

At the next screen, Windows 8.1 will tell you what it will do. Refreshing your computer *won't* delete any of your files, but you will need to reinstall your apps from the Windows Store (the Store will tell you which apps you have already purchased to make this easier). You will also need to reinstall any desktop software you have been using. The important thing, however, is that your files will be safe so long as they are stored in the main libraries and you haven't stored any somewhere else!

Creating a Recovery Drive

If your computer won't start at all, you can still Refresh it to get it working again. To do this, you first need to create a *Recovery Drive*. This is a USB flash drive that you can use to start your computer.

To create a Recovery Drive, search for *recovery* at the Start screen and run *Recovery* from the *Settings* search results. In the panel that appears, click/touch the *Create a recovery drive* link (Figure 12-6).

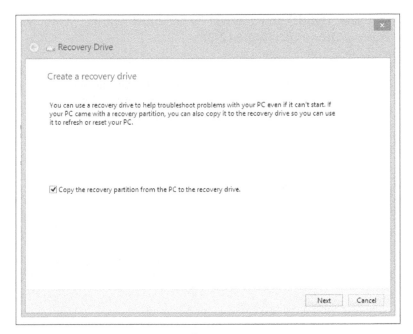

Figure 12-6. Creating a recovery drive

You will need to have a USB flash drive plugged into your PC, one that you're not using for anything else. If it is a large enough flash drive, and if your PC came with a Recovery Partition containing a copy of Windows 8.1 as provided by your PC's manufacturer, you can also copy across this backup copy of Windows 8.1 to the drive. This means that if Windows 8.1 won't start and you can't restore it from a backup image or a Refresh image, you can still restore it to how it was when you bought the computer.

 When purchasing a USB flash drive large enough to store the system backup copy of Windows that came with your computer, choose one that is 32GB or preferably 64GB in size.

Refreshing Windows 8.1 from a Recovery Drive

If you're in a situation where Windows 8.1 simply won't start on your PC and you need to reinstall the operating system, start the PC from the Recovery Drive you created **because you have created one and**

kept it safe, right!?) and you will be presented with the Windows recovery environment (Figure 12-7).

 If your PC is experiencing difficulty starting, you might find that it starts into the Recovery environment automatically. This will occur if Windows 8.1 fails to start three times.

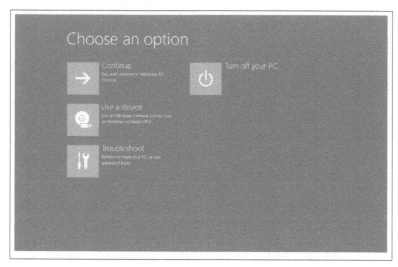

Figure 12-7. The Windows Recovery Environment

If you have started your PC from a Recovery Drive and you want to restore a backup image that was provided with your PC and that you copied to the Recovery Drive when it was created, click/tap the *Use a device* button and choose your USB flash drive from the options it then lists. If you are using Windows 8.1's own Refresh image, click/tap the *Troubleshoot* button.

At the next screen you will see a large *Refresh* button, click this to begin the recovery process. Be aware that this can take some time, so if you are using a laptop, ultrabook, or tablet, make sure it is plugged in to the electricity.

Using System Restore to Rescue Windows

If your computer is generally misbehaving but still starts, perhaps after you have installed a new piece of software, a new hardware driver, or an update, you can roll the system back to the point just before the recent change took place. To do this we need *System Restore*, which you can search for at the Start screen. A restore point is a snapshot of critical Windows files taken when an important system change is made.

Should something go wrong and Windows become unstable, you can click/touch *Create a Restore Point* and in the window that appears click/tap the *System Restore* button to find a restore point that was made recently and when your computer was running well. By clicking/touching a restore point and then clicking/touching the *Next* button, you can restore Windows files to this point. This does not affect your files and documents.

Maintaining Windows 8.1

So far, this chapter has focused on backing up and restoring Windows and your files, should disaster strike. But ideally, you just want to keep Windows 8.1 running smoothly so that problems don't occur, right?

Well, Windows 8.1 is able to perform maintenance tasks on itself. You can access this feature by searching for *maintenance* at the Start screen and clicking *Change automatic maintenance settings* in the *Settings* search results.

In the window that appears, you have just two options (Figure 12-8). When does automatic maintenance run and can the computer be woken up to run it? This second option will only work if the computer is set to Sleep rather than shut down, and if it is plugged in. If this is unlikely, then try setting maintenance to run at a time when you will often be using the computer, such as in the evening. Maintenance won't prevent the computer from working and it won't stop you from doing what you are doing.

Figure 12-8. Changing the Automatic Maintenance Settings

The maintenance tool will clean up unwanted temporary files that accrue during daily use of your computer, perform diagnostic tests, and make sure your security and Windows Updates are up to date. This really is a great solution because it takes all of the hassle out of keeping your Windows 8.1 computer running smoothly.

You can always check the *Windows Update* settings manually in PC Settings, and indeed I would recommend you do this now and again, but the automatic maintenance of Windows 8.1 should provide all the peace of mind that you need.

Summary

Windows 8.1 is great at maintaining itself, but in the event that something *does* go wrong, all is not lost. If you only or predominantly use Windows 8.1 apps and not desktop software, the *Refresh* option is a great way to get Windows working again when it misbehaves. Sometimes, though—for example, after you've just installed a Windows update—you will know that the PC is misbehaving. In this case, a simple System Restore will commonly fix the problem.

If disaster strikes, then you're still not out of options. It's wise to create a *Recovery Drive* and a System Image copy of Windows 8.1 if you have enough spare hard disk space for one, either on an external USB hard disk or on a second internal hard disk in your computer.

You should *always* make sure you keep regular and up-to-date backups of your files. This is by far the most important thing you can do on your computer. If you can also try to keep a copy of your files outside of your home, perhaps in an Internet service such as Microsoft's Sky-Drive, it will help protect your files should the worst happen and you suffer a theft or a fire.

There have been a lot of tips in this chapter for keeping Windows 8.1 running smoothly, and in Chapter 13, I'm going to share with you even more top tips for getting the maximum benefit out of Windows 8.1.

More Top Tips for Using Windows 8

Throughout this book, I've shown you how to do the things that you'll most commonly want to do with your Windows 8.1 computer. But what about all the other cool stuff that makes using your desktop PC, laptop, or tablet *really* easy? In this chapter, I'll share with you my favorite tips and tricks for getting Windows 8.1 to work for you, and for making your Windows 8.1 computer a really fun thing to use.

Use a Picture Password

Windows 8.1 practically begs you to log into your computer using a Microsoft Account. This does have some big advantages, such as automatically setting up your email, calendar, Internet favorites, and the Windows Stores for apps, music, and videos. To keep yourself secure, though, you will need a strong password, and I'll show you how to create one in the next section of this chapter.

Typing a long password into Windows 8.1 every time you want to use the computer can be annoying, so why not create a picture password instead? You can choose any picture on your computer and use it to unlock your computer by touching and tapping it. The actions you can choose from include tapping the picture, drawing straight lines on it, and drawing circles. You can create a Picture Password from the main screen of PC Settings.

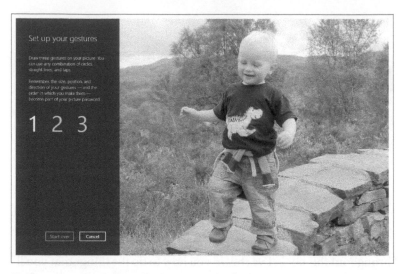

Figure 13-1. Creating a picture password

Picture passwords can be every bit as secure as a regular strong password because they can seem completely random. In Figure 13-1, you will see a picture of Gilbert and you might tickle his tummy, poke his nose, draw a line between his hands, or draw a circle around his face to unlock your computer.

Use a Secure Password

Picture passwords aside, I would always advise that you use strong passwords for everything else, such as your email, websites you visit, banking, and so on. Here are my top tips for creating a really secure password.

A really secure password should be at least 12 characters in length. Consider the following tips as well:

- Use a mixture of upper- and lowercase characters, numbers, and symbols.

- Substitute some numbers and symbols for letters. (e.g., 5 or $ instead of s or S, or 1 instead of i or L, and () instead of 0.

- Use a code you'll remember, such as capitalizing the second or third letter of each word.

- String words together to make a strong core password that you can use for everything.

- Mix into your core password, perhaps at the beginning or the end, the first few letters of the website or service you are logging into to make that password unique to that service.

- Check how secure your password is at *http://www.howsecureis mypassword.net*.

Use Libraries in Windows 8.1

Windows 8.1 comes with some standard folders for your Documents, Pictures, Music, and Video, but these are limiting in that you can't move them (at least not easily), and your files will remain resolutely stuck on the same physical hard disc on which Windows 8.1 is installed. While this isn't generally a problem, especially if you keep a backup copy of your files, it can be a problem if something goes seriously wrong and Windows 8.1 needs to be reinstalled.

The answer to this is Libraries, which you can turn on in File Explorer by clicking the *Navigation pane* button on the *View* tab in the Ribbon. Check *Show libraries* to enable the feature (Figure 13-2).

Figure 13-2. You can enable Libraries in File Explorer

The Libraries will then appear in File Explorer and will appear to be the same as your Documents, Pictures, Music, and Video folders. This is because they are just that, but they're also more configurable. When you are viewing a Library in File Explorer, a *Library Tools (Manage)* tab will appear on the ribbon (Figure 13-3). Click this for access to the *Manage Library* button. This displays a window that allows you to add extra folders and hard disks to the library, and it also allows you to change the default save location. You can use this feature if you want to store your files on a different disk than the one on which Windows 8.1 is installed.

Figure 13-3. You can manage Libraries in File Explorer

Reinstall all Your Apps in One Go

If you need to Refresh your PC (Chapter 12) or you are using Windows 8.1 on a new PC, you can install all of your previously downloaded apps in a single action. When you are in the Windows Store, open the App Bar and click the *Your Apps* button near the top left of the screen. All of your apps that are not currently installed on the PC will be displayed, and you can install them all at the same time here.

Get Extra Information from the Start Screen

The Live Tiles on Start Screen Apps are a great way to get lots of information about a wide range of subjects, all really quickly and at a glance. You might not find a general use for a Finance app, for example, although its Live Tile might also be able to give you helpful information about currency exchange rates.

 You can search within an app by opening, for example, *Search* from the Charms menu to search for new games or other software in the Windows Store.

Bookmark Web Pages and App Information to Read Later

If you see something online or in an app that you'd like to read or look at further, but you simply don't have the time, you can bookmark it. To do this, open the *Share* charm and from the options that appear click/tap *Reading List*. This saves the content to a separate app where you can get easy access to it later.

 Not all apps are compatible with the Reading List, and in order to read web content later you will need an active Internet connection.

You can then access whatever you have saved in the *Reading List* app, available from the Start screen (Figure 13-4). Here everything that you've saved will be listed for access whenever you like. You can delete items from the Reading List by right-clicking/touching and holding them and then clicking *Delete* from the App Bar.

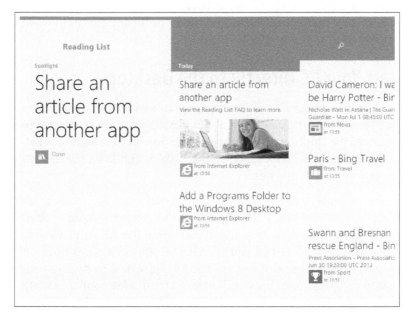

Figure 13-4. You can save many types of content with the Reading List

---

Make Sure You Keep Regular Backups

Your files, pictures, music, and videos are the most precious things you will *ever* keep on your computer, and it's essential to keep them securely and properly backed up. I showed you how to create backups in Chapter 11, but there are other tips I can offer.

I would always recommend that you keep two backups, one locally on an external USB hard disk (and these are very cheap these days) and another using a cloud backup service such as Microsoft SkyDrive, Amazon S3, Mozy, or DropBox.

You should always keep regular backups; once a month is usually best but you might want to keep them more regularly if you use your computer for college or work, or if you add or change files often.

If you can't use an Internet cloud backup service, perhaps you can keep a copy of your backup off site on a USB hard disk that you bring home once a month to update. Perhaps you have a USB hard disk you can leave with a friend or family member. This helps protect your files from fire, flood, and theft.

Don't rely on CDs and DVDs for backups. These can degrade over time, making them unreadable, and there's never any clue as to when they will fail.

Start Your PC Directly to the Desktop

If you want to primarily use desktop programs with Windows 8.1, you can bypass the Start screen when the operating system starts and go straight to the Desktop instead. To activate this, on the Desktop, *right-click* anywhere in a blank space on the Taskbar and from the options that appear click *Properties*.

In the options window that appears, click the *Navigation* tab (Figure 13-5), and check the box *Go to the desktop instead of Start when I sign in*. Optionally you can also force the All Apps view to display automatically when you click the Windows key (this turns off the Start screen), and you can tell the All Apps view to display your desktop programs first (the standard view is to display your apps first). If you check this option, you will also need to go into the All Apps view, click *by name* at the top left of the screen, and change it to *by category*.

Figure 13-5. You can tell Windows 8.1 to start directly to the desktop

 If you *really* miss the Start Menu from earlier versions of Windows, there are several ways either to restore it or get an alternative. The best place to start is *http://www.stardock.com*, which provides a wide range of Windows customization products. Another option is ViStart, which you can download from *http://www.lee-soft.com/vistart*.

Create a Custom Refresh Image

In Chapter 12, I showed you how to refresh your computer if it malfunctions. While this will restore Windows 8.1 to a fully working copy, you will have to reinstall all of your desktop software and apps afterward.

You can create a custom refresh image too that contains all your currently installed apps and desktop programs. A custom refresh image differs from the standard one included with Windows 8 in that it will include your user accounts and Windows settings. This can make getting up and running again after refreshing your computer much quicker and simpler, especially if you have changed time-consuming settings, such as Family Safety.

To create a custom refresh image, search for *command* from the Search charm, and in the results that appear, *right-click* on *Command Prompt* and select *Run as Administrator* (Figure 13-6). You will also need to click/touch *okay* on a security prompt.

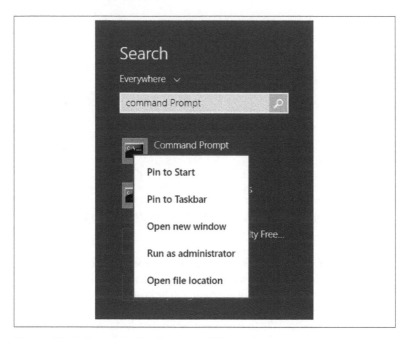

Figure 13-6. Opening the Command Prompt

In the window that appears, type the following two commands, pressing the *Enter* key on your keyboard after each one:

`mkdir C:\Win8Refresh`
This creates a new store folder for your custom Refresh image.

`recimg -CreateImage C:\Win8Refresh`
This creates a custom Refresh image for your copy of Windows 8.1.

You can also store the Refresh image on a second hard disk in your computer if you have one. This can make the system even more robust if something goes wrong with Windows. To do this, change the **C:** drive letter to the letter of the spare hard disk.

 When you buy a new PC, you should always keep all the disks and manuals that came with it safe and together in a dry place. A shoebox is usually a great storage box for these, and you should add any extra disks and documentation that you get with new hardware and software to this box when you buy new things for your computer. If you need to reinstall Windows 8.1 or if you want to upgrade your computer, you will often need these disks and manuals.

Using the Calendar and Clocks on the Desktop Taskbar

If you use your computer for work and use the desktop a lot of the time, there are powerful calendar tools you can access and you can set clocks for different time zones from your Taskbar.

To access the time and date functions in Windows 8.1, click/touch the time and date on the far right side of the Taskbar, and a date and time panel will open. Here's how you control it.

You can control the date panel by clicking the small left and right arrows above the calendar (Figure 13-7). These will move the calendar backward or forward a month. You can also click/touch on the month and year between the arrows to switch to different calendar views. This allows you to quickly move to different months and years.

Figure 13-7. The Date and Time Panel

You can add additional clocks for different time zones to this panel by clicking the *Change date and time settings* link at the bottom of the panel. In the window that appears, click/touch the *Additional clocks* tab and you can add up to two more clocks, specifying the time zone you want for each one.

Choosing the Programs that Open Files

If you find that a file is opening with the wrong program or isn't opening at all, you can fix this by searching for *default* at the Start screen and click/touch *Default Programs* when it appears in the search results. In the next panel, you have several options, including choosing what happens when you plug things in to your computer, such as USB flash drives, CDs, DVDs, and external hard disks (Figure 13-8).

Figure 13-8. The Default Programs Panel

To change the program or app a file opens with, click/touch the *Set your default programs* link. This will open a new panel where, on the left, you will see a list of all your installed software and apps. Find the program that you want to use as the default to open this particular type of file. For example, if you want to open music files in Windows Media Player, find *Windows Media Player* in the list and click/touch it.

In the right side of the panel, you can choose to set this program as the default for every type of file it can open, which in this case is music and video, or you can *Choose defaults for this program* instead, if perhaps you want to use it for music but not videos (Figure 13-9).

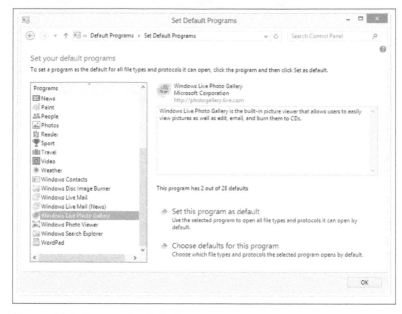

Figure 13-9. Setting the default program

Managing Your Default Sound Devices

If you find that sound on your computer isn't working correctly—for example, if you've plugged in headphones but the sound is still coming out of your speakers—it's easy to change the default sound device. To do this, go to the desktop and *right-click* with your mouse on the speaker icon next to the time and date on the Taskbar (Figure 13-10).

Figure 13-10. Opening the Playback Devices Panel

From the options that appear, click/touch *Playback devices* and this will open a new panel showing all the sound playback devices in or attached to your computer. To change the default sound device, click/

touch the device you want to use for sound and then click/touch the
Set Default button at the bottom of the panel (Figure 13-11).

Figure 13-11. Setting the default sound device

 When you have finished, you may need to set the
default playback device back to what it was origi-
nally so that you can continue to listen to sound and
music (e.g., if you switched temporarily from speakers to headphones).

Turn It Off and On Again

This is the perennial troubleshooting tip and the most commonly giv-
en piece of advice by computer professionals. If you find that something isn't working or is malfunctioning, just try turning everything
off and then on again. You'd be surprised how many times this fixes a
problem.

If you still have trouble, Windows 8.1 comes with some easy-to-use
automated troubleshooters (Figure 13-12). To find these, search for

troubleshooting at the Start screen and run *Troubleshooting* from the *Settings* search results.

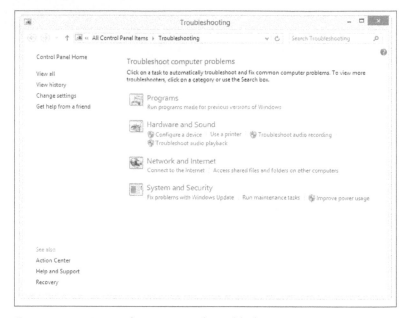

Figure 13-12. Using the automated troubleshooters

 Opening *Settings* from the Charms menu inside an app can reveal additional options for that app that will appear in the top right of your screen.

The automated troubleshooters are separated into categories such as *Programs* and *Hardware and Sound* to make it easy to find what you are looking for. Each troubleshooter takes you through a series of questions to help it diagnose and repair problems.

Summary

In this book, I've guided you through everything you need to get started with Windows 8.1. You can use your computer to have fun, share things with friends and family, or work and be productive. I hope you've found it helpful.

I offer additional help and support, including tutorial videos, all of which you can see at my website *http://www.thelongclimb.com*. If I were to finish this book with one simple piece of advice, it is this: you shouldn't panic when something goes wrong. Your computer still isn't as dependable as your microwave and can stop working or misbehave occasionally. Don't get duped into spending money on expensive technical support.

You can also find my help, how-to, and support app in the Windows Store, just search in the store for *The Long Climb*. I would suggest visiting my website or using my app for more help and working through the fixes and repairs to Windows 8.1 that I have detailed in this book.

Whatever you do with your computer, though, I sincerely hope you enjoy using Windows 8.1.

About the Author

Mike Halsey is the author of several Windows books, including *Troubleshoot and Optimize Windows 8 Inside Out* (Microsoft Press), *Beginning Windows 8* (Apress), and *Troubleshooting Windows 7 Inside Out* (Microsoft Press). He is a Microsoft MVP (Most Valuable Professional) awardee and a recognized Windows expert.

He regularly makes help, how-to, and troubleshooting videos, including in-depth masterclasses for people of any technical ability.

Mike lives in an eco-home in Sheffield (Yorkshire, UK) with his rescue border collie, Jed.

Get even more for your money.

Join the O'Reilly Community, and register the O'Reilly books you own. It's free, and you'll get:

- $4.99 ebook upgrade offer
- 40% upgrade offer on O'Reilly print books
- Membership discounts on books and events
- Free lifetime updates to ebooks and videos
- Multiple ebook formats, DRM FREE
- Participation in the O'Reilly community
- Newsletters
- Account management
- 100% Satisfaction Guarantee

Signing up is easy:

1. Go to: oreilly.com/go/register
2. Create an O'Reilly login.
3. Provide your address.
4. Register your books.

Note: English-language books only

To order books online:
oreilly.com/store

For questions about products or an order:
orders@oreilly.com

To sign up to get topic-specific email announcements and/or news about upcoming books, conferences, special offers, and new technologies:
elists@oreilly.com

For technical questions about book content:
booktech@oreilly.com

To submit new book proposals to our editors:
proposals@oreilly.com

O'Reilly books are available in multiple DRM-free ebook formats. For more information:
oreilly.com/ebooks

O'REILLY®